BILINGUAL SU

A practical approach for teachers

BILINGUAL SHAKESPEARE
A practical approach for teachers

Alex Fellowes

Trentham Books
Stoke on Trent, UK and Sterling, USA

Trentham Books Limited

Westview House	22883 Quicksilver Drive
734 London Road	Sterling
Oakhill	VA 20166-2012
Stoke on Trent	USA
Staffordshire	
England ST4 5NP	

First published 2001

British Library Cataloguing-in-Publication Data
A catalogue record for this book is available from the British Library

ISBN 1 85856 247 3

Photographs by Alex Fellowes

Designed and typeset by Trentham Print Design Ltd., Chester and printed in Great Britain by Cromwell Press Ltd., Wiltshire.

Contents

Dedication

This book is dedicated to the memory of Mary, my late wife, who was and will always remain a continual inspiration to me.

Acknowledgments

Many thanks to Joy Rice and Target Print for all the invaluable ICT support and guidance during the drafting process.

Also I am immensely grateful to Dr. Rex Gibson, editor of *Cambridge Schools Shakespeare*, for writing the Foreword to this book and for all the tremendous encouragement he has given me in my schools' Shakespeare work over the years.

Thanks are due as well to Monica Deb, Education Adviser for Ethnic Minority Achievement in Kirklees LEA, for being kind enough to proof-read the book and provide me with advice and constructive feedback.

Let me also express my approciation to the Royal Shakespeare Company's Education Department and most especially to Wendy Greenhall, its former director, and Fiona Lyndsey, co-worker, for all their help and encouragement.

I must not forget the wonderful pupils of Scotchman Middle School, Bradford, without whose amazing enthusiasm, flair and extraordinary ability this book would never have been written.

I must also make special mention of Peter O'Hare, with whom I collaborated on many of our school's Shakespeare performances and who provided such imaginative and memorable musical settings for the productions.

Foreword

It is singularly appropriate that Alex Fellowes begins his fine book with Cassius' prescient words as the Roman conspirators wash their hands in Julius Caesar's blood:

How many ages hence
Shall this our lofty scene be acted over,
In states unborn and accents yet unknown.

Even Shakespeare however could surely not have known just how successfully his language, characters, plots and themes would, hundreds of years after their creation, continue to seize the imagination of people all around the world. It is commonplace today to remark on Shakespeare's universal appeal. The unique achievement of Alex Fellowes is the flair with which he demonstrates how that appeal works in practice with bilingual pupils in the classroom.

Bilingual Shakespeare is a testament to the pioneering work that a gifted teacher has developed over three decades. It provides a rationale, a method, and a large number of helpfully detailed examples of successful school Shakespeare with bilingual pupils. Here is a very talented teacher who has put principles into practice, and who now provides genuine help for others to follow his trailblazing example.

Bilingual Shakespeare is acutely alert to language and to the importance of drama. It shows clearly that each Shakespeare play is a script, not simply a literary text. As such it is to be spoken, played with, and actively performed. That speaking, playing and performing is necessarily a social experience, and Alex Fellowes shows how well school Shakespeare succeeds when it is based on pupils working cooperatively together in pairs and groups of all sizes.

The special distinction of *Bilingual Shakespeare* is how it attests to the crucial principle of ownership. It shows how pupils from a British Asian background respond with heart-warming imagination and intelligence when a teacher gives them the opportunity to make Shakespeare their own. The book provides evidence that the key to successful school Shakespeare is to enable pupils to take possession of the plays and the sonnets by inhabiting them through their own language and culture. In demonstrating that ownership in action, Alex Fellowes' book is both an inspiration and a resource for all teachers.

Rex Gibson

1

Why bilingual Shakespeare?

How many ages hence
Shall this our lofty scene be acted over,
In states unborn and accents yet unknown.
(Cassius in *Julius Caesar*.)

B ilingual pupils from British Asian backgrounds respond enthusiastically to Shakespeare and his plays. I found that encouraging them to use their first language is a creative, exciting and effective way of working, and an ideal way of supporting their efforts to grasp his language, imagery, plots and characterisation.

This book describes how some of the plays were explored in the children's first language as well as English. It aims to:

- provide a clear rationale for any teacher who adopts a bilingual approach

- offer a practical teaching structure for delivering a Shakespeare play, which not only uses effective drama strategies and techniques but is enhanced and transformed by adding a bilingual dimension

- set out accounts of practical drama work on Shakespeare which successfully used a bilingual approach, thus providing models of good, effective teaching and learning.

So the book not only demonstrates the immense educational value of bringing bilingualism into the learning environment; it also provides evidence of the effectiveness of bilingual approaches, informed by

1

my own teaching of Shakespeare over thirty years. The result is this practical handbook for teachers wanting to adopt this rewarding teaching approach to Shakespeare. It considers why Shakespeare should be studied using a bilingual approach; what its educational advantages are and whether this approach is valuable only for bilingual students or whether it has wider relevance.

The answers to these questions are to be found under the following headings:

- Good educational practice
- The need to re-invent Shakespeare
- A question of pupil entitlement
- Providing new insights to Shakespeare's plays and language
- The appropriateness of South Asian languages
- The effectiveness of working within a storytelling framework

Good educational practice
When teachers confront children with literature from another era which still remains relevant today, it is important to give every pupil the opportunity to create their own meanings and develop a real sense of ownership of the original. They should have the chance to bring their personal life experiences, social contexts and cultures to their interaction with Shakespeare and his plays. As educators we have to enable our pupils to build bridges between what they already bring to the classroom from their homes and communities and the new learning in which they are actively engaged. By doing so we afford them status as learners and underline the value of their cross-cultural skills.

Since language is the prime vehicle for conveying and transmitting culture, it is essential for bilingual pupils to incorporate their own first language into the learning equation. In a multilingual environment, as a matter of good educational practice, encouraging bi-lingual skills is a learning imperative. But it is even more: language is also the means by which we express our personalities and unique-ness. To deny bilingual learners the choice of using their first

2

language is to deprive them of a fundamental means of expressing their individuality. Enabling pupils through active drama experience to convey their own insights in their exploration of Shakespeare's plays imbues their learning with a real sense of personal relevance, and language is the key that unlocks this learning process.

Diversity always enriches the learning environment: it never detracts from it. Shakespeare should be heard in many different voices, accents, dialects and languages. No-one, for example, could deny the power of Kurasawa's version of *Macbeth*, performed in Japanese and set within the cultural and historical background of a feudal Japan dominated by ruthless Shoguns and their warrior elite of Samurais. Transplanting Shakespeare's dark story of power, evil and corruption to a completely different culture gives an audience new insights into the dynamics of its plot, characterisation and universal themes. The language of Kurasawa's visual imagery, combined with the spoken language in the play, recreates the story in a fresh and compelling way.

Re-inventing his plays keeps Shakespeare alive

Re-inventing Shakespeare's plays in a range of appropriate languages and cultural milieu keeps his plots, language and characters vibrant. At a school level, it enables pupils to own them in a very real way.

Because Shakespeare tackled so many universal issues that transcend the normal boundaries of time and social convention, he provides anyone working with his plays with vast scope for reshaping and reinterpreting his ideas and language. When a bilingual class exploits the pupils' language skills to emphasise, for instance, the difference between the Montagues and Capulets in *Romeo and Juliet*, a new dimension is brought to the conflict between the two families. Having the Montagues speaking Panjabi or Urdu gives them a cultural identity and sharpens their dissension with the English speaking Capulets. This leaves space for contemporary issues related to race and culture to be brought into the frame and add dramatic edge to the story.

Shakespeare is exclusive to no age, class or cultural group. He belongs to everyone and speaks to people from every cultural, social and linguistic background.

A question of entitlement: customising Shakespeare

Another learning imperative is to ensure that bilingual pupils receive their full cultural entitlement. As well as having the opportunity to experience the rich and varied sources of Asian and world literature, music and art, they have a right to access the best in their English cultural heritage, and this includes the work of Shakespeare.

What I have found particularly exciting is the way that a cross-cultural approach to Shakespeare's works not only enables bilingual pupils to understand them better at their own level of personal experience but provides them also with the scope for blending eastern and western traditions. Combine this with using Panjabi, Urdu, Gujerati, Bengali, Hindi and so on along with English and one produces a potent dramatic brew.

Take the great Indian epic, the *Ramayana*, as an example. Rama's flight from a corrupt and hostile court, accompanied by his devoted wife, Sita, and his loyal brother, Laxman, into the dark and perilous jungle, has close parallels with Shakespeare's *As You Like It*. Shakespeare's heroine, Rosalind, also has to effect a desperate escape from a corrupt and hostile court, and is accompanied by her devoted cousin, Celia and her faithful retainer, the Fool Touchstone, to the Forest of Arden. That both parties of refugees find a safe haven, comfort and healing in wild, natural places considered forbidding and dangerous, enhances the similarities between the two plots.

In Shakespeare's *Cymbeline,* Posthumous' cruel rejection of the virtuous and faithful Imogen on the strength of the villain Iacomo's lies can be compared with the plot of another celebrated story from the Asian subcontinent, *Magnun and Laila*. Laila's selfless love is cast aside by the gullible nature of Majnun, her prince, who has been deceived by a conniving and wicked magus. Both heroines restore the situation through acts of personal courage and sacrifice.

Romeo and Juliet and its tragic account of two star-crossed lovers has many echoes in the famous Indian love story, *Hir and Ranja*, another story of forbidden love and family hatred and conflict.

Recently I was shown a traditional Panjabi story in which the aging Rani, having unfairly cast out her youngest and best-loved daughter, was turned out of her kingdom by her ungrateful sons. Her rejected daughter came upon her homeless mother in the forest and, disguising herself, took care of her, only later disclosing her true identity (rather like Edgar as 'Mad Tom' to his blind father, Gloucester). There are many similarities with Shakespeare's *King Lear* and the story could well inspire an alternative 'Queen Lear'.

The One Thousand and One Arabian Nights, tales written in early medieval times when the Islamic caliphate was at its cultural height, by an unknown author from Baghdad, is another source of stories and inspiration for a cross-cultural approach. The tales have much in common with Boccacio's *Decameron*, from which Shakespeare certainly drew. The Arabian Nights share many of the elements found in Shakespeare's plays: sibling rivalry, quests, disguise, deception, sorcery, enchantment, double-dealing, trickery, the supernatural and so on. Here, too, are 'stories within stories'. The genies in Aladdin would be at home on Prospero's island; the spirit Ariel is freed from a tree just as the genies are freed from the lamp and the ring. Both stories explore whether the spirits will be granted their freedom or whether their masters will continue wielding their magic powers. The Sultan Bilal has, like King Lear, a succession crisis: instead of three daughters, he has to choose between three squabbling sons. As with the Shakespearean king, he puts them to the test, but with a very different outcome. The question of inheritance and succession is one that preoccupies both writers and is worth exploring through drama. Also, both Shakespeare and the author of the Arabian Nights end many of their stories with a resolution, one that contains powerful and enduring lessons about life and the nature of human relationships.

Shakespeare was a great borrower of good stories. Had he had access to the wonderful treasury of tales from the Asian sub-continent and the Middle East, with their mazey plots, magic and fantasy, intrigue and evil machinations, and their strong, memorable characters, he would doubtless have drawn from them: so why can't we?

To cross-fertilise Shakespeare's plots with similar ones from South Asian sources is to customise his plays for pupils and audiences from these cultural backgrounds and to provide a means of re-interpreting them within a highly imaginative storytelling framework. This approach is rich in exciting and creative dramatic possibilities, something I return to later.

Providing new insights into Shakespeare's plays and language

By employing a bilingual drama teaching approach, a rich, dynamic language learning environment is created which affords all the pupils in a multilingual class a chance to discover the meanings of Shakespeare's words and imagery.

The monolingual pupils too, when exposed to such a rarefied language environment with its opportunities for code-switching and creative word play, are far more ready to accept the challenges of Shakespeare's dense language. The focus on Shakespeare's language becomes more intense and enhances the capacity on the part of the pupils to grasp its underlying meanings through the experiential medium of drama. Shakespeare's words need to be spoken out loud. When the spoken language is linked to activities which encourage them to search for comparable words and images from other languages, and to contrast styles of expression in different dialects and accents, pupils are given the means to develop new insights into his plays on their own terms. The more the sculptor works the clay, the more s/he can shape it to represent the idea s/he is trying to create. The more pupils can work the language of Shakespeare's plays in all its varied forms, the more likely it is that they can discover new meanings for themselves.

For language to be properly absorbed and understood, it has to be actively spoken and heard. Shakespeare was a playwright and actor – he wrote his words to be spoken, not paraphrased and dissected for the sake of some public examination. Good drama should provide the learning environment for this to happen. By enabling more than one language to be used, the teacher raises the language learning stakes and presents all the pupils with a range of new and fascinating challenges.

Working at so many language levels and registers, of which Elizabethan English is only one, empowers bilingual learners and enriches the learning environment for everyone.

The appropriateness of South Asian languages for working with Shakespeare

The majority of my bilingual pupils have Panjabi as their first language. This is their working language at home and in the community, alongside English. Their written first language is Urdu, however, in which a significant proportion are literate, some at a high level of attainment, gaining A and B grades in the GCSE each year.

Urdu is a poetic and literary language. I have done projects with groups in Year 8 working on the Urdu *ghazal*, the equivalent of Elizabethan sonnets. These poems, written to a particular poetic form and structure, originated in the courts of the Moghul emperors, some of whom wrote *ghazals* much as king Henry VIII wrote love ballads. *Ghazals* and sonnets shared many of the same elements: they were concerned with themes such as love – divine and human – mortality and the march of time, life and death. Working on *ghazals* in a multilingual class can provide the ideal springboard for cross-cultural activities; their affinity with Shakespeare's sonnets in terms of theme, imagery and form is striking. Bilingual pupils who can't use Urdu script but can speak the language can also access *ghazals*, by reading them in a Romanised, phonetic script.

Not surprisingly, Shakespeare translates well into Urdu. A good many of my bilingual pupils, through regular practice, have become skilful translators. They enjoy the challenge of finding words and images in Urdu that are comparable to language in a piece of Shakespearean text. This is a sophisticated and advanced skill and should be encouraged by any teacher working on Shakespeare with bilingual pupils. The effect of a Shakespearean soliloquoy translated into Urdu and performed for a bilingual audience can be nothing short of electrifying!

While Urdu can provide bilingual students with a beautiful and poetic mode of expression, actively using Panjabi in drama work can lend a Shakespearean scene a wonderful knock-about comical quality. Panjabi, as it seems to be developing in cities like Bradford or Birmingham, is changing under the influence of English. It is a flexible language, often borrowing at will from English when required. It is ideally suited for code-switching and is a lively vehicle for bilingual improvisation. I have found that bilingual pupils can move with consummate ease between the two languages in their role-play; they are also prepared to absorb a few Elizabethan expressions and vocabulary in their improvised code-switching if asked to or if the mood takes them.

Setting up a dramatic situation which directly follows the plot of one of Shakespeare's scenes as a basis for bilingual improvisation can produce extraordinary results, especially when you ask your students to use specific keywords and significant phrases from the original text. I personally find this a fascinating and innovative way of working. If bilingual improvisation of this kind is then structured into a piece of performance, the dramatic effect can be spectacular. By using Panjabi and their natural code-switching skills, pupils in role, for example, as the Shepherd Autolycus and his son in *The Winter's Tale*; or as Stephano, Trincolo and Caliban in *The Tempest*; or as the Mechanicals in *A Midsummer Night's Dream* can bring a bilingual audience to its knees! This was certainly the case in a production of *Henry IV Part 1*, in which I encouraged the pupil playing Falstaff to use Panjabi. He ended by inventing a first language dialogue for practically all the dramatic situations. The impact of the resulting comedy on our audiences was amazing. It proved the point that the appeal of fat Falstaff is universal, regardless of culture or language, and revealed Panjabi as an ideal medium for communicating Shakespearean comedy.

The ideal drama teaching structure
A storytelling approach to Shakespeare and his plays goes hand in hand with a bilingual one; they complement one another.

I've already mentioned how I and my pupils have experimented with blending South Asian stories with Shakespeare's, where there are notable similarities. This way of working can be extended considerably.

Stories appeal to everyone, whatever their age or culture, and Shakespeare was a master storyteller. Each of his plays has its own unique plot and story – in fact it often contains several. Many have double plots that weave in and out of one another. Within the plays, characters relate their own stories – stories within stories – for example, Prospero tells his daughter Miranda the story of their expulsion from Milan and their arrival at the magic island; the ghost tells his son Hamlet the story of his murder; Othello impresses Desdemona during their courtship with fantastic tales of what he's seen on his travels and the adventures he's had as a soldier.

With any group of pupils, the best and most effective way into a Shakespearean play is to treat it as a brilliant and vivid story. His plays have many exciting elements that can appeal to pupils: shipwrecks, tempests, ghostly apparitions, suicides, battles, duels, madness, disguise, intrigue, treachery, revenge, murder, magic, fairies, wizards, riots, assassinations, ferocious beasts, monstrous apparitions, slap-stick, Tom-foolery, mischief, double dealing, cross-dressing and mistaken identity, to name just a few!

When I'm working with a group of pupils on a Shakespeare play, I try to begin each new session by going into role as a narrator: introducing the important passages of the plot which we will develop, linking them together when necessary, and moving the story forward. I am using a device Shakespeare himself employs on a regular basis. The main characters in his plays constantly use reported action. I try to end each drama session on a cliff-hanger, in the hope of leaving the pupils excited and in suspense over what might happen next. In this way a Shakespeare play can become a serial thriller which engages the pupils, as active participants, in the unravelling of the story from crisis to crisis, dilemma to dilemma, while constantly maintaining a high level of dramatic tension.

This creative storytelling approach opens up a range of drama activities which can give pupils valuable insights into Shakespeare's characters and plots, and the issues he raises. With bilingual pupils, combining work of this kind with their use of first language greatly enhances the dramatic process.

The structure of certain of the plays even encourages teachers to experiment with pupils' language skills. *As You Like It* is an excellent example. Having Duke Frederick's court communicating in English, while the inhabitants of the Forest of Arden talk in Panjabi, highlights the contrast between court and country in Shakespeare's day. Achieving this contrast with language invests each social environment with its own culture – and in Elizabethan times court and country were different worlds, each with distinctive codes of behaviour and modes of expression. Providing a bilingual structure also enlivens the encounters between the court refugees like Touchstone and Jaques and the indigenous Arden inhabitants. The romantic misunderstanding between Rosalind, disguised as the boy Ganymede, and Phoebe, her hopeless admirer, for instance, can make greater sense to an audience, especially when Phoebe doesn't actually understand anything Ganymede is saying to her and is only responding to 'his' body language and gestures. Creating a language difference between the two means that the more passionately Ganymede tries to explain his true feelings, the more Phoebe will be encouraged to misread all the signals she's receiving. This can produce a new take on the comic situation.

A Winter's Tale is another play that lends itself to a bilingual approach. Having the Sicilians speaking in English while the Bohemians speak in Panjabi and Urdu sharpens the dramatic tension in the second half of the story and lifts the comedy. The sheep-shearing scene can be replaced with an Asian betrothal party accompanied by Bhangra music, for example, to enhance the new cultural atmosphere.

Creating such cultural relevance makes scenes like this far more accessible and understandable to pupils because it enables them to experience Shakespeare within the context of their own lives, culture and language. When Polixines, King of Bohemia, and Camillo, formally Leontes' chief minister, arrive in disguise at this re-designated event, they can make all their asides in English, describing their reactions (both are bilingual because they have spent much

'Autolycus', A Winter's Tale

time living in each country). Polixines' utter shock at his son Florizel's carry-on behind his back with Perditta (seemingly a mere peasant girl) is highlighted by using both English and Panjabi. This linguistic device builds up the dramatic anticipation when it comes to the point at which the King reveals himself to his son; all the while, Polixines had been encouraging Florizel in Urdu or Panjabi to describe his true feelings for Perditta and how he intends to keep his father totally in the dark about the matter. As the King is actively encouraging his unaware son to confide in him, he can speak what is in his mind in English in the form of dramatic asides. This increases the tension in this compelling situation, creates a heightened level of suspense and establishes a significant bridge for a bilingual audience.

In terms of the comedy in the play, making the dodgy dealer Autolycus bilingual seems obvious in a multicultural school. Here is a man of the world who has been around. Having Autolycus communicate with his fellow Bohemians in Panjabi, while constantly delivering asides to the audience in English about what he is actually thinking and plotting, is a perfect comic device. It enlivens all his exchanges with the gullible Shepherd and his son, and it offers the pupils a whole range of opportunities for developing comedy through their role-play.

In *Antony and Cleopatra*, the action takes place in two different countries, Rome and Egypt, and there is the added dimension of cultural and political conflict between east and west. This could provide drama teachers with the ideal theatrical context for staging a Raj play, with Cleopatra an Indian rani desperately trying to maintain the independence of her kingdom against the encroachments of British imperial power. If Cleopatra's palace used Urdu, like the Moghul court of the period, its cultural identity would be clearly established. Mark Antony would be portrayed as a British Viceroy who comes increasingly under the rani's spell. There is also a specific historical comparison upon which one could draw: the courageous and determined resistance by the Rani of Jhansi to British rule in the first half of the 19th century. Putting the play in this historical context also raises some interesting contemporary issues regarding Cleopatra's relationship with Antony.

Traditional Asian dress could add visual support, emphasising the flamboyant character of Cleopatra's court. Giving *Antony and Cleopatra* a historical and cultural perspective of this kind makes the play far more comprehensible, relevant and interesting to a bilingual community than locating it in Ancient Rome; it also capitalises on the linguistic and cross-cultural skills of the pupils.

Employing a storytelling framework when introducing pupils to Shakespeare and actively promoting language skills in a multi-lingual learning environment gives teachers enormous scope for re-inventing his plays and bringing his characters to life. We could speculate on what might have happened if, for example, Duncan had overheard Macbeth's heated argument with his wife before he went to bed on that fateful night. There are challenging dramatic possi-bilities in having Macbeth speak partly in English and partly in first language, so the King can only grasp snatches of the conversation. A similar effect could be produced in *Julius Caesar* if a foreign citizen who discovers the plot to kill Caesar can convey this infor-mation only through an interpreter – a task made even more difficult by the fact that Caesar is surrounded by Brutus, Cassius and their confederates on the steps of the Senate house.

Viewing vital moments in Shakespeare's plays through the eyes of minor characters is another highly effective means of reworking im-portant moments in the stories:

- What could the servants downstairs in the palace of Elsinore be saying about Denmark's royal family and all their goings on?

- What kind of conversation do the guests have after the banquet at which the ghost of Banquo appeared to Macbeth?

- How do Valentine and Duke Orsino's retainers react to the arrival of the young upstart, Cesario (alias Viola), who has in a matter of days become the Duke's soulmate and closest confi-dant? Or what might happen if a member of Illyria's secret service begins to investigate the recent and mysterious ship-wreck off its coast?

Injecting into all these hypothetical scenarios the relevant community languages and code-switching possibilities hugely enriches
the role-play for the exchange of secrets, the spreading of rumours,
the development of intrigue, the sharing of confidences, and the
creation of misunderstandings. A bilingual method of working
stimulates the pupils' improvisations and, through this linguistic
make-believe, can manufacture a seemingly endless catalogue of
human dilemmas and problems that characterise Shakespeare's
plays. Such dramatic experimentation enables pupils to touch upon
some of the fundamental dynamics underpinning the structure of
Shakespeare's works.

2
Drama techniques for multilingual classrooms

This chapter summarises the drama teaching techniques I've found particularly effective and which are referred to in the course of this book. In providing accounts of successful drama teaching practice, I have tried to show the advantages of using a combination of such techniques in each lesson. Children need exposure to a variety of learning styles. The teacher should always seek to ring the changes. Clear goals, specific deadlines, moments of reflection, sharing and listening to the ideas of others and gaining positive feedback are all vital elements in this process.

Each technique is illustrated with practical examples of how they might be used in a variety of Shakespearean contexts which also incorporate an added bilingual extension.

The advantage of having a multilingual class is that the pupils become one's greatest resource: using the special linguistic and cross-cultural skills they bring into school enriches and strengthens the learning environment for monolingual as well as bilingual children.

Technique: Hot-seating
Description:

- put someone in a specific role

- use the device of a chair or other object to signify the person in role

- invite the rest of the group to question the character's actions, past life, present aspirations, fears etc.

Example:

- hot-seat Richard III about his behaviour and actions

Bilingual extension:

- pupil in role, who is bilingual, speaks only in first language and through an interpreter. This provides opportunities for evasiveness and dramatic asides

Advantages:

- controlled, clear dramatic structure

- opportunities for teacher or pupils to go into role with minimum risk

- encourages analysis of character

- brings Shakespeare's characters to life

- stimulates discussion and raises issues

Technique: Teacher in role
Description:

- teacher taking on a specific role to lead or support whole group drama

- teacher has the choice of a variety of role categories:

    (a) the control figure e.g. Prince Escalus in *Romeo and Juliet*

    (b) the devil's advocate e.g. Jacques in *As You Like It*

    (c) the manipulator e.g. Iago in *Othello* or Puck in *A Midsummer Night's Dream*

    (d) the underdog e.g. Macduff's wife in *Macbeth* or Hermione in *The Winter's Tale*

    (e) the agent provocateur e.g. the Fool in *King Lear*

    (f) the outsider e.g. Caliban in *The Tempest* etc

Example:

• teacher goes into role as Julius Caesar, surrounded by Brutus, Cassius and their conspirators as they prepare to murder him

Bilingual extension:

• the conspirators can use first language to express their inner thoughts, doubts and intentions during this dramatic exchange

Advantages:

• teacher can influence the drama from within

• teacher can act as a catalyst to the dramatic action – challenging thinking, supplying information, posing problems, asking questions, encouraging reflection etc

• teacher can become an equal participant in the drama and act as a fellow learner rather than a judge

Technique: Tableaux

Description:

• ask pupils to catch the moment by putting themselves into a still picture

• several stimuli can be used for this activity: photographs from newspapers, stills from videos, reproductions of paintings, pieces of text, comics and visual novels

Example:

• pupils working on *The Winter's Tale* have to imagine how an artist might have depicted the moment when Hermione is sent to prison by Leontes, her jealous husband, and forcibly separated from her son, Mamillius

Advantages:

• controlled and focused activity

• plenty of opportunity for group discussion and negotiation

• often produces a highly satisfactory outcome

• promotes reflective feedback

Technique: Montage
Description:

- a natural extension of the tableaux activity

- creating a series of still frames that convey a sequence of events

Example:

- pupils make a tableau representing a photograph taken from a professional production of, say, the shipwreck scene in *The Tempest*.

- they reconstruct this tableau so that it depicts the same group of people ten minutes before this event takes place

- they produce a final tableau illustrating what has happened ten minutes after the main action

- they can then run the three different frames together like an animated film

Bilingual extension:

- the passengers or the crew on the ship talk a different language. Pupils put words to their three tableaux and develop them as improvisations with the language difference as a prime focus. This heightens the dramatic tension

Advantages:

- builds upon a dramatic structure the pupils already know

- accesses pupils to visual texts and allows them to use these as stimuli for drama work

- provides opportunities for developing other aspects of drama: dialogue, movement and even dance

Technique: Thought tracking
Description:

- having made tableaux, pupils are encouraged to speak their thoughts at that frozen moment in time

Example:

- moment after Gloucester has been blinded, everyone in the tableaux must say what they are thinking or feeling

Bilingual Extension:

- the servants and guards in the scene express their horror and fears in first language

Advantages:

- adds dramatic depth to tableaux and montage work

- provides tableaux with language

- promotes individual reflection

- enables the re-enaction of violent scenes within a controlled framework

- encourages even the quietest, most reticent pupils, requiring them only to contribute a sentence or just a single word

Technique: Mime

Description:

- re-enact a piece of dramatic action without words, often accompanied by a spoken narrative

Example:

- a silent film depicting the assassination of Julius Caesar or the farcical ending to the *Comedy of Errors*

Bilingual extension:

- during the mime, the teacher freeze-frames the action at significant intervals and pupils comment on the proceedings in their first language as well as English

Advantages:

- a particularly effective device if incorporated in a performance to a bilingual audience

- opportunities for the quieter and less forthcoming pupils to play a leading part

- develops non-verbal skills e.g. gesture, facial expression, movement, dramatic shape

- acquaints pupils with a popular Elizabethan dramatic form: the dumb show

Technique: Forum theatre
Description:

- small group of pupils are put in role and begin acting out a dramatic situation

- rest of the group are observers but with the power to stop the action at any time and make changes, suggest dialogue or propose new dilemmas and developments

Example:

- the court scene in *The Merchant of Venice* up to the moment when Shylock demands his pound of flesh. Pupils do not know the outcomes and have to help the actors develop the drama

Bilingual extension:

- Shylock will only communicate in first language, even though the court knows he can speak their language. His legal representative is bilingual. This allows for more conferring, raises the level of resentment towards Shylock himself and slows the drama down. It also sharpens the cultural divide between Shylock and the Venetians and provides an opportunity to examine the issue of racism in the play. Using the convention of forum theatre, it gives bilingual pupils the chance to intervene in the course and development of the drama, wearing the mantle of experts

Advantages:

- everyone is involved either as an actor or observer/director

- encourages creative thinking and problem solving

- makes pupils reflect critically on issues such as dramatic shape and form

- everyone has a stake in the drama

Promenade theatre

Description:

- taking a dramatic scene, dividing it into different components and sharing these out among the pupils, who are organised in groups

- teacher or pupil goes into role and takes their character around each of the groups

- the drama takes place wherever the character in role has arrived

Example:

- it is the night before the Battle of Agincourt. The pupils are all English soldiers, squatting around the camp fires discussing tomorrow's battle and their chances of success or survival

- each group is given an additional dramatic focus e.g. a dying soldier; someone on a charge for theft and possibly facing execution (so who are the real enemy?); a critically ill child back at home, etc

- after the pupils have developed their individual improvisations, the teacher goes round from group to group as Henry V in disguise, putting the soldiers' loyalty to the test while having his own decision for undertaking this war challenged

- as the teacher does this, the other groups act as an audience to the dramatic action

Bilingual extension:

- some of the soldiers are Welsh and will only talk in their first language through an interpreter; they are militantly pro-Welsh and are only there because they need the money and have no prospects in their native country (again it raises the question – who are the real enemy?)

Advantages:

- extremely versatile dramatic structure
- encourages pupils to utilise space more effectively
- introduces pupils to a novel mode of performance
- involves the pupils in a varied and interesting range of drama activities that require listening as well as speaking

Technique: Tunnels of conscience, doubt, guilt etc

Description:

- putting a teacher or pupil in role and asking them to confront and respond to their personal dilemma or situation
- individually, everyone else must challenge the character in role with either a question or a statement about an aspect of their personal dilemma. For this purpose they form a human tunnel through which the main protagonist has to walk.
- the character in role then responds to each individual challenge as he/she proceeds through the tunnel

Example:

- whole group goes into role as Macbeth's conscience just before he sets out to murder Duncan
- each person must say something for or against this action, in the form of a statement or a question

Bilingual extension:

- on the sidelines, three or more bilingual pupils are put into role as the Weird Sisters, who taunt Macbeth in first language every time he responds to his conscience in the tunnel. If the pupil in role as Macbeth is also bilingual, he can reply to them in first language. This device can produce an intriguing and dynamic improvisation which operates at a number of interesting dramatic levels

Advantages:

- creates a real dramatic atmosphere
- builds personal commitment to the drama
- invests the drama with special significance
- provides a means for pupils to suspend disbelief

Technique: Mood walk
Description:

- pupils find their own space and, on a signal, walk independently to represent a given mood, reflecting the inner feelings of their character

Example:

- a class reproduces the atmosphere of fear and suspicion at the court of Richard III
- they draw lots to determine beforehand who will be the king's spies
- the spies are given an instruction about how they can recognise a fellow spy (some subtle modification to dress, perhaps).

Bilingual extension:

- teacher ensures that the pupils who draw the lots as spies are bilingual
- they are instructed to talk to one another only in their first language. This intensifies the atmosphere of conspiracy

Advantages:

- activity demands that the pupils think about what they are doing
- develops non-verbal skills
- flexible dramatic device
- encourages total participation
- can be used in response to text
- creates dramatic tension

Technique: Reportage

Description:

- translating a passage of Shakespearean plot into the style, form and language of modern media

- this can take the form of news reports, press conferences, TV debates, chat shows, Jerry Springer-type presentations

Example:

- King Lear, his daughters and his sons-in-law (with Edmund in the wings!) have to appear on the Jerry Springer Show to discuss the problems of their disfunctional family

Bilingual extension:

- the royal family are permitted to use their first language and code-switch if at any time they want to exclude the TV presenter and audience. This can create some wonderfully comic moments, especially when many in the audience can understand the first language asides and outbursts

Advantages:

- imbues a sense of realism in the drama

- gives the pupils a vehicle for communication which they are all familiar with and enjoy

- stimulates debate and discussion in a contemporary framework of issues which are as relevant today as in Shakespeare's time

Technique: Interview, interrogations, counselling and so on

Description:

- using a contemporary mode of questioning or examination to explore a Shakespearean character in greater detail

Examples:

- therapy for Romeo or Juliet

- interview for 'Cesario' (alias Viola) upon 'his' arrival at Duke Orsino's court

- marriage guidance for Othello and Desdemona

- police interrogation for Macbeth and his wife after Duncan's murder

- industrial tribunal for Malvolio against his employer because of unfair treatment

- psychiatric examination of Iago (echoes of Hannibal Lecter!)

- an enquiry into the shipwreck in *The Tempest*

Bilingual extension:

- the bilingual subjects speak their words in English but their thoughts in first language. This makes for an extremely thoughtful activity and adds depth to the drama

Advantages:

- invests a piece of improvisation with a sense of authenticity

- provides a usable and flexible structure

- encourages pupils to devise appropriate questions for a range of situations

- helps pupils put themselves into the shoes of a Shakespearean character and bring it to life

Technique: Ritual

Description:

- pupils submit to an established pattern of movements and an agreed formula of words, both of which are invested with great significance

- a definite ritual and protocol must be established beforehand – and possibly practiced – as well as a written declaration

Example:

- pupils go into role as King Lear's family and household warriors, who must renew their oaths of loyalty to the aging king

Bilingual extension:

- Lear's daughters, who are bilingual, must express their thoughts in first language after their formal declarations of loyalty before the test of love. These first language asides thus take on the character of Shakespearean soliloquies.

Advantages:

- creates dramatic atmosphere
- builds personal commitment to the drama
- invests the drama with significance
- provides a means for pupils to suspend belief

All these techniques are deployed in the following chapters, along with appropriate bilingual extension.

Falstaff

3

Hamlet, the bilingual Prince

amlet proved to be one of the most successful bilingual drama projects I've worked on. Colleagues were sceptical about my tackling this play with twelve year olds, but why not?

Hamlet is a young person with a lot of attitude, who has a dodgy and extremely troubled royal family. The play is full of contemporary issues: handling grief and loss (publicly and privately), sleaze and corruption in high places, betrayal, making choices, the nature of madness, and unrequited love. And it has the added appeal of the supernatural. For twelve year olds its undeniable attraction is that the central character's young person is rebellious, amusing and unpredictable, fighting against the odds and the establishment.

One wedding and a funeral
A state funeral and a marriage run into one another at the beginning of the story, so from a dramatic point of view the best way in for the pupils is this:

• begin with pupils in groups of eight producing a tableau which depicts the recent funeral of the late king

• ensure that Gertrude, the Queen and Hamlet's widowed mother, the King's brother Claudius, Hamlet himself, and Chief Minister Polonius are all depicted

- let the pupils decide how they must be arranged, paying particular attention to physical posture and facial expressions. Others in the picture assume the roles of friends, relatives or guards

- the same groups create a tableaux of the marriage between Gertrude and Claudius less than two months later, giving special attention to Hamlet's outlook

- groups reform tableaux and, on an agreed signal within the group, move from the funeral picture into the marriage tableau.

The contrast between the two is unfailingly striking, and highlights the main cause for Hamlet's grief and anger at the outset of the play: these tableaux are a physical representation of this reality.

- Next, all the groups make their still pictures for a third and last time, but with each participant, whether a major or a minor character, deciding what they might be saying at that instant (like the 'speech bubbles' in a cartoon)

- everyone has to limit their spoken words to one sentence

- on a signal, each member of the tableau makes their statement in sequence

- everyone then decides upon their thoughts in that frozen moment of time

- bilingual pupils speak their thoughts in first language.

In royal courts, what is spoken and what is thought can be entirely different matters.

Bringing different voices and different languages into this dramatic form invests the individual contributions with something that is more intimate and, significantly, more secretive. It can also introduce an unexpected element of humour into such formal proceedings. Using Panjabi to do this is often amusing and it raises the level of audience response from the monolingual as well as bilingual pupils. This working framework enables all the pupils to gain greater insight into the personal agendas of the different characters in the play.

When the groups combine these elements in the form of a mini-performance, a striking dramatic effect can be achieved without much effort. Tableaux are an accessible and focused drama activity. Although the final product is non-verbal, there is much group discussion at the planning stage and everyone has the chance to contribute their ideas. Pupils are also introduced to some basic principles relating to theatrical shape.

Thought-tracking and the addition of different languages raise the dramatic stakes further. Each group watches the others' contributions, providing the teacher with an opportunity to invite discussion and reflection, for example:

'The person acting Hamlet in that tableau, what did you feel towards your mother at that moment at the funeral?'

'Does anyone have any ideas what else might have been going through his mind?'

'What do you think Claudius is thinking? What are his feelings towards Hamlet?'

'The person in the role of the lady-in-waiting at the wedding, what do you think she might have whispered to her friend nearby about the whole situation? Why would she have been afraid to be overheard?'

'What effect did Hamlet have on you at the wedding when he said what he did in Panjabi? Why did some of you want to laugh?'

This direct and active drama approach engages the pupils from the outset in the key issues and conflicts in the play and challenges them to project themselves into the minds of the main characters and the other characters witnessing these events in Elsinore. This all helps the children to transport themselves into the world of Elsinore. It makes the behaviour of all those who inhabit this world more understandable. Pupils also have to make important dramatic choices in more than one language.

Hamlet's grief

At this stage, I'd want the pupils to explore more fully the nature of Hamlet's grief and appreciate his growing sense of anger and isolation. My starting point for this would be the court at Elsinore and its seemingly insensitive attitude towards Hamlet's feelings. It can be done like this:

- Pupils spread themselves around the room, finding their own space

- they walk round in a purposeful businesslike manner, doing their best to ignore one another, carrying a message or going to an important meeting

- at one given signal, pupils commence their mood walk and, at another, they freeze.

Once an atmosphere has been created in which everyone is pre-occupied with their own immediate tasks and interests, a pupil assumes the role of Hamlet.

- Hamlet sits on chair in the middle of the room

- upon a signal, pupils recommence their mood walk, but this time moving around the Prince

- at another signal, the courtiers freeze again and Hamlet is asked how s/he feels

- on a flip chart or OHP, details of Hamlet's behaviour at the beginning of the play are written up. This would include some of the following:

  his choice of black clothes

  his miserable attitude and countenance

  his refusal to participate in court life and festivities.

The scene is repeated, but this time with the pupils whispering to one another about these highlighted aspects in the Prince's behaviour. Again Hamlet describes how he feels.

His responses to this have included:

'I didn't like being talked about behind my back... I felt threatened... I felt very alone, without any friends... I was getting more and more angry... I wanted to shout........ I hated every-one.... I felt everyone was against me...'

- All the courtiers are given cards on which are unsympathetic statements. For instance:

'Hamlet, we are all sorry that your father died, but isn't it time to move on in your life?'

'Hamlet, your father died nearly two months ago, don't you think you have grieved enough?'

'Hamlet, can't you think of your mother's feelings for a change? How does she feel when she sees you dressed like this and moping round the palace all the time?'

'Hamlet, I know you lost your dad, but can't you at least share your mother and uncle's joy and try to hide your grief for their sake?'

'Hamlet, crying won't bring your father back...'

'Hamlet, would your father have wanted you to keep all this up?...Everyone understood why you were so upset at first but surely enough is enough.'

'Hamlet, don't you understand who you are in the kingdom? Why not do as your uncle wants? Be more of a man and set a better example to your subjects'.

- mood walk re-established, but this time pupils approach Hamlet one at a time and deliver their statements; the Prince responds to each of them

- the bilingual pupil in role as the Prince replies to all the courtiers in first language, so creating greater dramatic effect.

Having a bilingual pupil in the Prince's role means that his feelings can be expressed in another language, demonstrating his growing sense of anger and alienation to the whole situation in a more personal way.

The statements that the courtiers direct against Hamlet mirror the words Claudius himself uses at the beginning of the play:

> *Tis sweet and commendable in your nature, Hamlet,*
> *To give these mourning duties to your father.*
> *But you must know your father lost a father;*
> *That father lost his; and the survivor bound*
> *In filial obligation for some term*
> *To do obsequious sorrow. But to persevere*
> *In obstinate condolement is a course*
> *Of impious stubborness. Tis unmanly grief.*
> *(Act 1 Scene 2 ll 87-94)*

Cold comfort, indeed, from the new king to his nephew and new son-in-law!

This is the signal to move on to the next phase in the drama: working on a piece of Shakespearean text in the context of the previous activities.

- Divide this speech into one-liners
- share these lines out among the pupils and then repeat the mood walk as before, but with the courtiers approaching Hamlet in the correct sequence and pronouncing Claudius' words
- Hamlet responds if he chooses to.

Using the actual text to build on all the improvisation work, and the feelings generated by it, helps to put a piece of Shakespearean text in context and gives the pupils a structure and a reference point for bringing it to life. The negative words used by the King to describe Hamlet's grief can be identified – obsequious, obstinate, impious, unmanly – reflecting the totally unsympathetic attitude of Claudius to Hamlet's natural grieving process. This activity also enables the pupils to deconstruct Shakespearean text and grasp its underlying meanings.

Hamlet's anger: O that this too sullied flesh would melt

Not surprisingly, Hamlet isn't only in deep sorrow about his father's sudden and unexpected death, he is also feeling bitter about people's reactions to it, most notably his mother's. He expresses this bitterness and anger forcefully in this famous soliloquy, and is explicit about the reasons for it:

> *O that this too sullied flesh would melt,*
> *Thaw, and resolve itself into dew;*
> *..............................O God, O God*
> *How weary, stale, flat and unprofitable*
> *Seem to me all the uses of the world!*
> *...............That it should come to this –*
> *But two months, nay, not so much, not two!*
> *So excellent a king that was to this*
> *Hyperion to a satyr; so loving to my mother*
> *That he might not permit the winds of Heaven*
> *Visit her face too roughly. Heaven and Earth*
> *Must I remember? Why, she would hang on him*
> *As if increase of appetite had grown*
> *By what it fed on. And yet within a month!*
> *Let me not think on't. Frailty, thy name is woman!*
> *A little month, or e'er those shoes were old*
> *With which she followed my poor father's body*
> *Like Niobe, all tears, why she, even she...*
> *Would have mourned longer – married with my uncle,*
> *My father's brother, but no more like my father*
> *Than I to Hercules. Within a month,*
> *Ere yet the salt of most unrighteous tears*
> *Had left the flushing in her galled eyes,*
> *She married. O most wicked speed...*
> *It is not, nor it cannot come to good.*
> *But break, my heart, for I must hold my tongue.*
> (Act 1 Scene 2 ll 129-159)

• Break this long passage into one-liners and share them out

• have the pupils organise themselves into the right sequence and speak their lines one by one, while standing in a large circle

• have them mix themselves up in the circle, then walk while speaking their lines to the next person in the sequence.

Having to synchronise movement with Shakespeare's language breathes life into it and gives it some physicality.

- Pupils highlight the most important phrase in their line. Their choices would look something like this:

  'Flesh would melt'
  'Resolve itself'
  'O God!'
  'How weary'
  'All the uses of the world'
  'Should come to this'
  'But two months'
  'So excellent a king!'
  'Loving to my mother'
  'The winds of Heaven'
  'Heaven and Earth!'
  'Must I remember!'
  'Appetite had grown'
  'Yet within a month'
  'Frailty, thy name is woman'
  'A little month!'
  'My poor father's body'
  'Why she, even she!'
  'Married with my uncle!'
  'My father's brother!'
  'Within a month!'
  'Most unrighteous tears'
  'Her galled eyes!'
  'Most wicked speed!'
  'It cannot come to good!'
  'But break my heart!'

- Pupils memorise these phrases and find their own personal space in the area

- closing their eyes, they visualise the human statue that would best represent their phrase

- on a signal, they make this statue

- in fours (following the sequence in Hamlet's speech) they devise group tableaux, using their chosen statues

- In sequence, the tableaux form and the pupils pronounce their phrases one by one

- this activity is repeated, but this time with all the bilingual pupils translating and saying their phrase in first language

- the whole group reflects on the difference made to the performances by the use of another language.

Working with a single phrase, chosen by the pupils as a result of their personal understanding of an individual line in a whole Shakespearean passage, makes what would otherwise be a daunting task achievable, meaningful and great fun. It also becomes a collective and co-operative process where every student has the opportunity to participate in an essentially physical activity, which in dramatic terms helps to make Shakespeare's language come alive in more than one language. Once again we have an ideal structure within which students can deconstruct a dense piece of Shakespearean text on their own cultural and linguistic terms and arrive at their own personal meanings.

Hamlet encounters the ghost of his father

Hamlet's confrontation with the ghost of his dead father is pivotal to the development of the plot; for pupils who have no previous knowledge of the story it is an intensely exciting and engaging moment – something that the teacher can exploit to the full, for example:

- Teacher goes into role as Horatio and models his encounter with a pupil in role as the Prince

- Horatio relates to Hamlet the terrifying experience he'd suffered on the battlements the night before, which the Watch had witnessed two nights together – how in the dead waste and middle of the night they had seen the ghost of Hamlet's father

- in role, the teacher uses phrases employed by Horatio in the original text, for example, that he saw:

A figure like your father...
Armed at all points...
With solemn march...
(and those of us who watched) almost to jelly with the act of
fear,
stand dumb
Once metought it lifted up its head as if to speak
But even then the morning cock crew loud
And at the sound it shrunk in haste away
And vanished from our sight...
(Act 1 Scene 2 ll 199-220)

• ascertain the reaction of the pupil in role as Hamlet, then stop the drama

• ask all the pupils how they would have reacted and record their responses on OHP or flip chart

• in pairs, pupils act out their own improvisations, predicting the outcome of the conversation; bilingual pupils do this in first language

• bilingual pupils perform their role-plays; the rest of the group work out their outcomes.

Giving pupils the challenge of predicting the ways in which Shakespeare's characters might respond to a dilemma or situation enhances their understanding of their subsequent actions.

The pupils are now ready for the moment when Hamlet encounters the ghost of his father.

• Dividing into three groups and making circles, the pupils go into role as the ghost

• three pupils go into role as Hamlet in the middle of these circles

• maintaining the secrecy of the ghost's disclosure, each pupil is provided with a small part of the text, the ghost's story

• display on pieces of card some of the lines from this text. Making Shakespeare's language so visible can support such an activity very effectively

Sleeping within my orchard, my custom always in the
afternoon
Upon my secure hour thy uncle stole
With juice of cursed hebenon in a vial
And in the porches of my ears did pour the leprous distilment
Thus was I, sleeping, by a brother's hand
Of life, of crown, of queen at once dispatched
Cut off even in the blossoms of my sin
No reckoning made
With all my imperfections on my head
If thou hast nature in thee, bear it not!
O horrible, O horrible, O most horrible!
Adieu, adieu, Hamlet. Remember me!
(Act 1 Scene 5 ll 59 ff)

• one by one the ghosts approach Hamlet, gradually unravelling to themselves and the Prince the dreadful nature of his father's death.

The unfamiliarity and density of Shakespeare's language is ideally suited to the purpose of this activity. All the pupils in role as ghosts sound otherworldly, creating a dramatic distance between themselves and Hamlet. What they are actually saying to Hamlet might not be immediately understood, which in turn prompts him spontaneously to ask leading questions, such as:

'He poured something in my father's ear? But I don't understand what that was! Can you repeat what you just said?'

Because of the difficulties of Shakespeare's language, most of the pupils won't have a clear idea of what happened in the orchard or its implications for the ghost, but each will possess a fraction of the picture. This is exactly what the teacher wants: a mystery that needs solving.

After seeing some of the groups in action, the whole class is asked what they thought the ghost was trying to say to Hamlet:

'Was he murdered? Who by? In what way? Something poured in his ear while he was sleeping? A juice? What kind of juice?

Hebenon? What do you think that is? How was it poured? In a vial. What do you think that is?' and so on.

An interesting extension to this scene is for the pupils to pretend that it has been decided to hold an enquiry into the late king's death. Investigators are sent around Elsinore to gather information and evidence. They have to interview a wide selection of people, including the Prince himself.

'How would they react to Hamlet's extraordinary evidence? Would anyone believe him? How would Claudius react, and how would the widow Gertrude?'

It could be that foreign investigators had been invited to pursue the investigation because they would be more objective and less intimidated than Danish subjects, since this was a possible murder enquiry involving Denmark's royal family. The detectives would use first language and work with the assistance of bilingual translators. This procedure adds tension to the role-play and makes the subsequent improvisations more thought-provoking and interesting. The language difference also creates a significant distance between the investigators and the investigated. (Incidentally one of Agatha Christie's famous detectives – Poirot – is bilingual!)

Ophelia and Hamlet: the issue of eavesdropping
At a time of intense grieving and mental turmoil, Hamlet would surely turn to his closest friends and the woman he loved. In Ophelia, sadly, he does not have a person who is sufficiently independent of her family to give him the love or support he needs. Her brother Laertes, who has just left for university, has warned her against becoming too close to the Prince, and her father Polonius is totally hostile to the relationship.

Ophelia's predicament raises issues regarding conflicting loyalties within families – between matters of the heart and family responsibilities and parental expectations. When this is also emeshed in the complexities of a royal court and all its intrigues, the issue of eavesdropping becomes an important factor in the development of the drama. I'd approach this in the following way:

- Before exploring Hamlet's relationship with Ophelia, set up a real life situation in threes in which two friends are talking behind the third's back but in their hearing

- look at a selection of these scenarios and use them as a basis for discussion: asking, for example, 'How much more painful is it for someone to overhear something said about them than being told to their face? What does it feel like?'

- model the same situation, this time with two bilingual pupils using their first language to exclude their monolingual friend and pass comments about him or her. The whole group reflects and comments on the issues this raises.

From this, move to the scene in which Ophelia, under pressure from her father, has broken off the relationship with Hamlet (what disastrous timing, given the Prince's emotional state!) and is returning all his presents (even worse timing!), while Polonius and Claudius eavesdrop on the whole encounter.

- In groups of four, pupils go into role as one of the characters

- pupils in role as Hamlet and Ophelia receive this text:

HAMLET
The fair Ophelia! (to himself)
OPHELIA
Good my lord,
How does your honour for this many a day?
HAMLET
I humbly thank you, well, well, well.
OPHELIA
My Lord, I have remembrances of yours
that I have longed long to redeliver.
I pray you now receive them.
HAMLET
No, no, I never gave you aught.
OPHELIA
My honoured Lord, you know right well you did,
and with them words of so sweet breath composed
that made the things more rich. Their perfume lost,

Take these again; for to the noble mind
Rich gifts wax poor when givers prove unkind.
There, my lord! (giving them all back)
HAMLET
Ha, ha? Are you honest?
OPHELIA
My Lord.
HAMLET
Are you fair?
OPHELIA
What means your lordship?
(Act 3 Scene 1 ll 91-108)

- the Hamlets and Ophelias highlight the lines that show they are upset and hurt and, in Hamlet's case, angry, so that when they read these lines they'll do so with heightened feeling

- teacher goes into role as Hamlet and models this exchange with a pupil in role as Ophelia, demonstrating maximum indignation

- pupils then act this out mirroring the same feelings but this time they develop and finish the argument using their own words.

There is much to be gained from using a short passage of Shakespearean dialogue as a stimulus for imaginative role-play. It also tests the pupils' understanding of the characters and how they respond in different situations.

- All the Polonius and Claudius characters eavesdrop this argument and whisper to each other from their hiding places

- review a selection of these role plays and highlight the good ideas and best elements; also offer constructive suggestions for improving them

- pupils return to their fours and polish their improvisations based on this discussion

- groups are instructed that at the point reached in their improvisations, Hamlet becomes aware that they are being overheard. How does this change his attitude?

- all the bilingual Hamlets use their first language to cut out the two eavesdroppers. How would this change the situation? How does this affect Hamlet's feelings and behaviour?

- pupils then see the outcome of the argument on film (the film versions featuring Mel Gibson and Kenneth Branagh are both very accessible).

Again, using the pupils' bilingual skills provides the teacher with more options for developing and deepening a passage of drama. This kind of activity also emphasises the value of group work. Pupils learn much from their peers, especially from the very able. For the less able, collaborating with them can offer the conceptual and linguistic scaffolding which can help in developing their own language and cognitive skills.

Feigning madness; Hamlet's game plan

The theme of madness runs through the play – feigned by Hamlet (although sometimes one is left guessing about this) and real in the case of Ophelia's breakdown.

Pretending to be mad becomes Hamlet's chosen strategy for enabling him to gather proof regarding the murder of his father by his uncle; by this means he hopes Claudius will drop his guard because he'll no longer take his nephew seriously.

Pupils hugely enjoy the experience of acting as if they were mad but they have a tendency to overact. It is important to provide them with a framework within which they can channel their role-play in a focused way, for example:

- set out four different areas in which pupils could develop their feigned madness:

    manner of dress

    manner of speech

    content of talk

    physical mannerisms

- in groups, pupils brainstorm specific types of behaviour, for each category, that will convince someone like Claudius that he was losing the plot

- everyone works in pairs in a situation where one person is a psychiatrist and the other Hamlet. Drawing upon previous brainstorming, the Hamlets put their mad acts to the test and try to convince the psychiatrists that they are truly mad

- in the feedback, everyone selects their best moment in their interviews. Pupils make qualitative evaluations of their work. Having them focus on a narrowly specific piece of drama action and dialogue directs their energies in a purposeful way

- teacher informs pupils that a hidden video camera has been recording their interviews and, on the play signal, they will re-play their chosen moment. On another signal, they will freeze frame.

This is an excellent way of sampling pupils' drama work. And it effectively models the best ideas produced from group discussions and subsequent improvisations.

- Ophelia's description of Hamlet's strange behaviour is passed round:

My Lord as I was sewing in my chamber,
Lord Hamlet, with his doublet all unbraced,
No hat upon his head, his stockings fouled,
Ungartered, and down-gyved to his ankle,
Pale as his shirt, his knees knocking each other,
And with a look so piteous in purport
As if he had been loosed out of Hell
To speak of horrors, he comes before me...
He took me by the wrist and held me hard,
Then goes he to the length of all his arm,
And with his other hand thus over his brow
He falls to such perusal of my face
Long stayed he so.
At last a little shaking of my arm,

and thrice his head thus waving up and down,
he raised a sigh so piteous and profound
that it did seem to shatter all his bulk
And end his being. That done, he lets me go,
And, with his head over his shoulder turned,
He seemed to find his way without his eyes,
For out of doors he went without their help,
And to the last bended their light on me.
(Act 2 Scene 1 ll 78-101)

- teacher leads shared reading activity, building on group discussions and drama work. Pupils underline or highlight examples of Hamlet's eccentric behaviour

Because of all the preliminary work, in which the pupils had to use their own imaginations to project themselves into Hamlet's efforts to play the madman, they will come to this text with a heightened sense of understanding and awareness.

- In pairs, pupils mime some of these behaviours

- in groups of five or six, improvise a situation described on a role-play card. Pupils in role as Hamlet act out their eccentric behaviour in a variety of dramatic contexts

- the cards would include the following:

Hamlet is summoned to the King – who will request his help in entertaining some foreign ambassadors

Polonius, in the company of some of the royal servants, complains about the appalling state of his bedroom

Gertrude, along with some of the royal dressmakers, tries to persuade Hamlet to wear fashionable and more colourful outfits than the black clothes he insists on wearing

- each group prepares for Hamlet's arrival, planning how they might handle the wayward and unpredictable prince.

To create a successful improvisation, thinking time needs to be provided (in a real-life Elsinore such discussions would surely have taken place).

- While each of the groups is occupied in the planning process, all the pupils in role as Hamlet are instructed to mix their repertoire of odd behaviour with utterings in first language expressing their anger towards Polonius and Claudius.

Shakespeare presents to us Hamlet as a scholar prince who would in normal circumstances have gone off to a German university: a youth who would have been fluent in at least one other European language. Suddenly ranting in another language might well have been an option for him in demonstrating his madness, and would prove a most disruptive dramatic device.

Whenever I've had bilingual students engaged in this improvisation, the Hamlets who have drawn upon their bilingual skills have injected into the role-play an exciting element of unpredictability, humour and conflict – so energising the entire dramatic sequence. This produces an atmosphere charged with confusion, anger and, in some cases, near-anarchy. This is how Hamlet's behaviour impacts on those around him. By exploiting the linguistic diversity of bilingual pupils, this atmosphere can be evoked in open role-play.

'The Play's the thing
Wherein I'll catch the conscience of the King'
The arrival in Elsinore of the travelling players provides the Prince with the opportunity he has been waiting for to lay a trap for Claudius and have the Ghost's story confirmed. This passage of the play also provides the drama teacher, who has the added resource of a multilingual class, with a range of varied and exciting possibilities, for example:

- in groups, some pupils go into role as the characters on the top table: Claudius, Gertrude, Polonius, Ophelia and Hamlet. The Hamlets are bilingual

- all the pupils in role as the players are issued with a set of instructions from Hamlet, describing the mime they must act out

- the instructions would go something like this:

    Enter a King and Queen

The King offers her some flowers: the Queen receives them affectionately

The King then lays himself down on a bank of flowers

The Queen, seeing him asleep, leaves him

Then another comes creeping into the garden, takes off the King's crown and kisses it

This person takes a small vial from his pocket and pours it into the King's ear, then exits

The King dies in terrible pain

The Queen returns, finds the King dead and collapses in shock and grief

The poisoner returns and comforts the Queen, appearing to share her grief

Later the murderer woos the Queen with flowers and gifts

At first she is unwilling to receive them

- the players put together their mimes to the accompaniment of a narrator who speaks in first language, because these actors are from a foreign country

- Hamlet translates the narrative for the top table with great dramatic emphasis

- the royal party react accordingly

This is kept as open-ended as possible. The bilingual pupil in role as Hamlet has the perfect opportunity to rub salt into the wounds of Claudius (and possibly of Gertrude) and exacerbate the king's growing sense of guilt and discomfort.

- The best improvisation is then used as a model and stimulus for forum theatre, in which the watchers are encouraged to stop the action at significant points and offer suggestions to which the actors must respond.

Forum theatre is an effective way of securing everyone's active involvement and promoting constructive analysis. Pupils have the chance to influence the development of a Shakespearean scene according to their own perceptions and ideas. It is also a very empowering exercise because these ideas and skills can be carried over to future improvisations.

All these strategies, tried and tested in my own teaching, can provide teachers with useful guidance for a way in, through active drama experience, to a Shakespearean play. Following the framework provided in this chapter, the rest of the play can be developed, focusing on key moments such as Hamlet's encounter with his mother and Polonius' death; Ophelia's descent into madness and suicide; Hamlet's exile and homecoming; the conspiracy between Laertes and Claudius; and the final duel.

In a day's workshop with a group of bilingual pupils in the fifth and sixth years, I put a different slant on the drama work by arriving in role as William Shakespeare and informing everyone that I wanted to change the final scene and needed their help to re-write it. This provided a strong sense of challenge to the workshop and an engrossing finale, in which several endings were proposed and then acted out.

4

A successful bilingual approach to learning the plays of Shakespeare

In my thirty years of teaching I've worked in schools in which as many as 90% of pupils come from a bilingual South Asian background. Outstanding lessons have taken place in several schools on the plays and stories of Shakespeare. I shared some of these as models of successful practice in the drama workshops I led at the Royal Shakespeare Company's Prince of Wales Summer School in 1999. I hope they will offer useful guidance for any teachers wanting to use a similar bilingual approach.

Othello: **The palace of rumours**
Target group: Year 8
The focus for this drama activity was the inner torment raging in Othello's mind, which expresses itself in his growing sense of paranoia and the corroding effect of jealousy on his ability to reason.

My aim was to get a class of thirty twelve year olds to recreate his workplace, the Governor's Palace in Cyprus. I wanted them to turn this into a hot-bed of conflicting rumour.

- As a warm-up, the class was divided in half, with one group creating a tableau depicting a palace that was honest, open and welcoming. The other group, by contrast, created a palace where courtiers were two-faced, scheming, sly and backbiting. This produced striking images that emphasised the comparison between the two types of group behaviour.

The pupils knew the story up to the point when Iago began to sow the seeds of doubt in Othello's mind about his wife's friendship with the young Cassio.

- Remaining in their two groups, half the pupils wrote complimentary comments about Desdemona and Cassio on slips of paper. The rest wrote comments which were critical and derogatory. The pupils in each group ensured that their comments were varied: they could be as unfair or partisan as they wished. They were also informed that it didn't matter if their comments agreed with somebody else's, because in the drama that might help to confirm a particular opinion about the two characters.

- One pupil went into role as Othello.

- Taking on the role of narrator, I declared:

  'You are all officers and courtiers in the Lord Othello's palace in Cyprus. There are rumours spreading about the Governor's wife and Cassio. Some are good but others are bad.

  I want you all to move about, a little nervously. As you pass someone, show some courtesy and perhaps exchange a polite greeting. On no account be rude or try to wind up the other courtier.'

- A slow movement from Vivaldi's Four Seasons accompanied their mood walk; they froze when the music stopped.

- The music began again, and as each passed a fellow courtier, they exchanged their comment for or against Desdemona and Cassio. Each time they did so they moved off smartly to the next person. They could register a certain measure of approval or disapproval, but always with the restraint expected in such a formal court. Vivaldi's music helped set the tempo and mood for the activity.

- Still as narrator, I told the class the following:

  'Othello's palace is in Cyprus. Othello is fluent in Italian, but perhaps not in the language of his Cyprus court, which would be Greek. I would like everyone who can do so to translate their comment into their first language or another language (for instance, French).'

- The pupil in role as Othello walked into the two groups of courtiers. The courtiers demonstrated great respect as they passed him, but exchanged their comments with one another in first language if possible, so the Governor would not understand anything that he might overhear. And the odd key word in English was muttered, to make the Governor feel even more uneasy.

- The music was suddenly switched off and all Othello could hear was the buzz of intimidating gossip and rumour.

- The court processed again and, as well as exchanging gossip in first language, individuals approached Othello and shared their comments with him. In this highly controlled environment in which everything happens at a slow and measured pace, Othello is bombarded with rumours and comments – some negative, others positive. Around him are groups of courtiers, whispering and secretly passing on items of gossip to one another.

- The effect on the pupil playing Othello was to make him feel surrounded by an unpleasant of web of rumour and conspiracy. Even though Othello is told a good many positive things about Desdemona and Cassio, it is human nature for him to dwell only on the negative, especially in such a conspiratorial environment. Having the pupils exclude the Governor by using their first language intensified his sense of isolation and vulnerability.

Othello dangled on a line: evil Greek chorus
Target group: Year 8

Here I wanted the same class actively to explore a piece of text in the play and deal head on with the issue of evil, as personified by Iago, the most plausible of all Shakespeare's villains.

The text I selected for the purpose was the following:

OTHELLO
But I do love thee, and when I love thee not,
Chaos is come again

IAGO
My noble Lord.
OTHELLO
What dost thou say, Iago?
IAGO
Did Michael Cassio, when you wooed my lady,
Know of your love?
OTHELLO
He did, from first to last. Why dost thou ask?
IAGO
But to the satisfaction of my thought,
No further harm.
OTHELLO
Why of thy thought, Iago?
IAGO
I did not think he'd been acquainted with her.
OTHELLO
Oh yes, and went between us often.
IAGO
Indeed?
OTHELLO
Indeed? Ay, indeed. Discernest thou aught in that?
Is he not honest?
IAGO
Honest, my Lord?
OTHELLO
Honest? Ay honest.
IAGO
My Lord, for aught I know.
OTHELLO
What dost thou think?
IAGO
Think, my Lord?
OTHELLO
Think my Lord? By heaven thou echoest me
As if there were some monster in thy thought
too hideous to be shown! Thou dost mean something.

I heard thee say even now 'I liked'st not that!'
When Cassio left my wife. What did'st not like?
And when I told thee he was of my counsel
In my whole course of wooing, thou cried'st 'Indeed?' '
And did'st contract and purse thy brow together
As if thou then had'st shut up in thy brain
Some horrible conceit. If thou did'st love me,
Show me thou thought!
IAGO
My Lord, you know I love you!
(Act 3 Scene 3 ll 92-121)

- To emphasise the way Iago so often echoes Othello, the class was organised into pairs. Standing opposite one other, the pupils took turns acting as the other person's reflection in a mirror.

- This was taken further: one made a statement while the other repeated the last word. This proved an effective device for preparing the pupils for the textual activity.

- In fours, two of the pupils took on the roles of Othello and Iago while the other two became their echoes, repeating the last couple of words in each line. With Iago's lines, this produced the effect of a double echo. It gave the script reading a very eerie feeling.

- The echoes, now in groups of four, wrote down what Iago might be thinking, in the margin of the script. If possible, these thoughts should be translated into first language.

Shakespeare, like most playwrights of his time, was preoccupied with the inner speech of his characters. Iago spends much of the play involved in an inner dialogue. Shakespeare touched on an area of human behaviour that is significant in an individual's intellectual development. Vygotsky (1978) has argued that speech turns inwards and becomes inner speech, interacting with and influencing the thinking and learning process. Building on this common Shakespearean device is to involve one's pupils in an intellectual process that is a significant element in their own conceptual development. Doing this in the first language of bilingual pupils can stimulate and activate a linguistic and cognitive operation which is essential to their individual learning.

- Iago's echoes were then collected together and formed them-selves into a chorus in which they repeated, as before, things that were said by both characters. In addition, they spoke out loud their previously devised malicious thoughts of Iago, sometimes in English and sometimes in their first language.

- Next, the chorus animated their words with movements; they were given the opportunity to decide and practice these move-ments beforehand.

The value of an approach of this kind to accessing Shakespearean text is that it involves a whole class at several different levels. It also gives pupils the opportunity to engage with the text itself and develop new meanings for themselves.

Producing a chorus as a means of expressing Iago's hidden evil in such a concrete and physical sense proved extremely effective. It was also acquainting the students with a dramatic form which originated in the earliest Greek theatre.

Having the pupils accomplish all this in Urdu or Panjabi invested the final product with a great deal of power, creating again an other-worldly atmosphere that came across as sinister and threatening.

Macbeth: an uninvited guest at the banquet
Target group: Year 5

Working on *Macbeth* with a class of bilingual nine year olds was an exciting experience. Especially memorable was the lesson in which the children re-enacted the unwelcome visit of Banquo's ghost to the Macbeth's dinner party.

- In groups, the pupils made tableaux depicting the murder of Banquo by Macbeth's hired assassins and also showing his son Fleance's escape.

- Dividing into two large groups with pupils in role as Macbeth, Lady Macbeth and the guests, two pupils became Banquo's ghost, waiting in the wings for their cue to enter.

- In each group an empty chair was placed for Banquo's ghost.

- In the meantime two raised platforms had been made. These elevated the six pupils given the roles of the Weird Sisters so they could overlook the action.

- A ritual was established for each of the guests when entering the banqueting chamber and being formally welcomed by the King and Queen: one pupil was made the caller and all the guests were given invitation cards stating their titles (e.g. Lord Ross of Strathclyde, Lady Mckenzie of Forfar etc). The caller read out the names and titles in order. The guests filed in and were greeted one by one with due formality, and ushered to their seats by the head servant.

- The pupils in role as Macbeth were handed a speech of welcome:

'I would like to extend a very warm welcome to all our guests.

Thank you all for travelling such long distances to share this special banquet with me and my wife, the Queen.

We are honoured by your presence.

I notice that our principal guest, my dear friend Lord Banquo, is still not with us.

In his absence, please raise your glasses to........Lord Banquo: may he enjoy a long life.'

Again, a useful ritual brought out the irony in the situation.

- At this point, the Banquos walked in and took up the empty chairs. It was understood that Banquo was invisible to everyone except Macbeth. Macbeth had no chair himself, so he was offered the empty one. The improvisation developed from this point, and it closely follows Shakespeare's plot.

The innovation in this scene was the Weird Sisters. It was also agreed that only Macbeth could hear their comments (no-one was supposed to be able to see them, not even the king).

- The Weird Sisters taunted and teased Macbeth as the scene developed, speaking in their first language.

This proved an effective strategy because it identified them as a group apart from everyone else (again with that other-worldly dimension) and injected humour into the exchanges with the King. The pupils understood that it was appropriate to use another language in this context, because most Scottish people would have spoken Gaelic at the time.

Once the guests fully understood the conventions under which they were operating and contracted themselves into the drama on these terms (they can't see or hear Banquo or the Weird Sisters), the improvisation developed its own fascinating impetus. The constant heckling by the Weird Sisters, combined with Macbeth's responses, which the guests thought were directed at them, was poignant and entertaining. And the incessant misunderstandings caused by Macbeth's replies and reactions to the Ghost produced some farcical moments. For example, when the King shouts at Banqo's Ghost to 'go away!' all the guests start to leave. To which Macbeth screams at them 'No! I didn't mean YOU!' By the end of the scene the guests didn't know whether they were coming or going. And all the time Lady Macbeth was making desperate efforts to silence her husband before he gave the game away.

Interweaving the dynamics of a typical Shakespearean scene with a set of clearly perceived rituals, and then introducing a dramatic device which brings another language into play, provides the chemistry to produce drama of the highest quality – achieved by a group of nine year olds!

Henry V at the gates of Harfleur: union militancy
Target group: Year 9
In an after-school drama club of former students, a new slant was given to one of Shakespeare's most celebrated scenes: Henry V endeavouring to rally his flagging troops at the siege of Harfleur. This was part of some performance work being prepared on the history plays for a local drama festival.

I explained to the pupils that most of Henry V's archers were Welsh and probably wouldn't have spoken English, so that anything the King wanted to say to them before the final attack needed to be translated.

- Students set the scene by creating a tableau of exhausted, de-moralised and home-sick Welsh soldiers, some of them suffering from severe stomach cramps (dysentery hit Henry's army hard during this campaign).

- In small groups, the archers grumbled amongst themselves in their first language. Possible subjects for their grumbling were suggested, such as the quality of the food, the back-pay still owing, the need to be back home helping on the farms, the fool-hardiness of the King's military adventure and, as Welshmen, what was in it for them anyway!

- A pupil in role as the sergeant eavesdropped upon the archers. At an appointed signal, he/she assembled them and brought them to task for all their whinging and their unfair criticisms of the King at a time when they should all be pulling together. This was done in first language. The subsequent argument set every-body thinking and in the mood for the next activity: the arrival of good King Hal himself.

- The King was confronted with the problem of communicating his uplifting speech through an interpreter, the Sergeant. The student in role as the King had constantly to stop for his speech to be translated. The soldiers replied to each of Henry's declara-tions with comments, criticisms or demands of their own. These were translated by the Sergeant to the King, who either carried on regardless with the speech or answered back.

The exchange went something like this:

KING HENRY V
(Act 3 Scene 1 ll 1-8)

Once more unto the breach, dear friends, once more

Why should we? You've already made us attack those damned walls five times! We're too exhausted now. We need to rest ourselves...and never mind the dear friends bit. We're soldiers – we're certainly not here by choice!

Or close the wall up with our English dead!

Oh notice, he says English dead! What about all the Welsh dead, or don't they count! I'd like to know what he'd do without us Welsh archers in his army. Maybe this isn't our struggle at all!

In peace there's nothing so becomes a man as modest stillness and humility

Peace! That would be nice – a chance to spend some precious time with my wife and kids instead of tramping half way across France in this disgusting weather!

But when the blast of war blows in our ears,
Then imitate the action of a tiger

And who got us into this wretched war in the first place? You, the King.
Imitate the action of the tiger! Fancy words! Let's see how you want us to do that – show us how to do it! Lead from the front!

Stiffen the sinews, conjure up the blood

Give us a half decent meal and we might be able to have enough energy for a fight.
We haven't eaten properly for days! How do you expect soldiers to fight on an empty stomach?

Disguise fair nature with hard-favoured rage

We'll give you rage! Why haven't we received all that back-pay you were promising us? You're asking us to sacrifice our lives for you, but you expect us to do it all for nothing.... and we're not even English! Shall we talk about money first?

The end product was remarkably exciting, with a variety of languages and registers being used in a fascinating interplay between performers and Shakespearean text: Elizabethan English, everyday English (used by both the interpreter and the King when he is forced to reply to the heckling by his troops), Urdu and Panjabi were all brought into play. The interpreter also had to come to terms with the meaning of the text if he/she was going to communicate its sense to the other soldiers. The original scene as devised by Shakespeare is, by this means, fundamentally changed. It is transformed into a trade union style negotiation between management and workers, in which the King cannot depend on rousing rhetoric to get what he wants; he has to address the grievances of the soldiers if he wants them to fight on his behalf.

Using the bilingualism of the students once more provided all the participants in the role-play with a structure filled with exciting dramatic opportunities for reworking and manipulating Shakespeare in fresh and innovative ways that made the meaning of the scene clear to a Year 9 class.

Romeo and Juliet: running the emotional gauntlet
Target group: Year 8

The famous balcony scene presents many challenges for drama teachers. Work with four large groups of 8th Years was developed into some highly charged romantic encounters.

- One pair of boys and another of girls went into role respectively as Romeo and Juliet.

- The Romeos were given Juliet's words:
  Tis but thy name that is my enemy.... to...Take all myself.
  (Act 2. Scene1 ll 80 – 90)

  The Juliet's were given Romeo's soliloquy:
  It is my lady, O, it is my love.
  that she knew she were!
  to
  That I might touch that cheek!
  (Act 2. Scene1 ll 52 – 66)

- The Romeos and Juliets worked out their reactions to these words of love and recorded them in the margins of the text.

- One pupil from each pair spoke in Urdu while the other echoed the words in contemporary English.

This collaborative work afforded a supportive framework in which ideas could be shared and pressure minimised.

- Meanwhile, the rest of the class formed two groups. Each group was given one of these two speeches. They were broken into one-liners, shared out among everyone and then practised in the correct sequence.

- The two groups made human tunnels. The Romeos travelled through the tunnel delivering the Juliet speech, and visa versa. One by one, the pupils in the tunnels rose, as each pair passed by and pronounced their lines.

The exchange took this form:

JULIET
Tis but thy name that is my enemy
Yes, the fact I'm a Montague doesn't bother her.

Thou art thyself, though not a Montague
Eh, she loves me for who I AM!

What's Montague? It's not hand, nor foot
Wait, what is she trying to say now?

Nor arm, nor face, nor any other part
Belonging to a man. O, be some other name!
But I thought it didn't matter that I was Montague. Now she wants me to change my name! I can't win!

What's in a name? That which we call a rose
By any other word would smell as sweet
Brilliant! I think she's comparing me to something really nice, never mind that my family are her greatest enemies.
I think she could love me after all!

This structure generates spectacularly effective results. It encourages the pupils to offer thoughtful responses to Shakespeare's language, particularly when the first language – Urdu – is used; it breaks up a long piece of text into manageable parts; it makes it participatory for all the students regardless of ability or English language experience (no-one is outfaced by too large a passage of text); and, because it is a collective exercise, it removes any potential embarrassment between the sexes when the pupils are confronted with one of the most intimate and passionate encounters in the play. As a result, the pupils are liberated to focus on the beauty of Shakespeare's actual words and images.

Once again, the students are asked in both languages to make an active and sensitive response to Shakespeare's language, and gain a real sense of ownership of the whole process when they do.

'Ill met by moonlight': Titania and Oberon's confrontation
Target group: Year 7

A memorable lesson with four classes in Year 7 was centred around Titania and Oberon's acrimonious meeting in *A Midsummer Night's Dream*.

To facilitate the drama activity I first mined the text. For this exercise I chose two speeches: Oberon's in Act 2. Scene 1 ll 74–80 and ll 118–121 and Titania's in Act 2. Scene1 ll 81–117

The grievances they aired in these speeches were listed:

Oberon's grievances:

1. Titania's love for Theseus – using her powers to break faith with Ariadne and Antiopa

2. Behind his back, absconding with the son of an Indian princess and making him her changeling boy and lavishing all her affections on this child, affections which should be reserved for him, her husband.

3. It is her duty now to hand over the Changeling Boy to be his personal servant.

Titania's grievances:

1. Oberon cheating on her with the amorous Phyllida and the Amazon queen Hypolyta.

2. Because of his unreasonable and hypocritical jealousy ('the forgeries of jealousy') taking it out on the world around them by:

    producing contagious fogs
    cutting out the warmth and light of the sun
    flooding all the fields

'Oberon' Midsummer Night Dream

spoiling the harvests

making all livestock food for carrion birds

causing whole-scale famine and death

encouraging the spread of disease

taking away 'all winter cheer'

creating a world devoid of music, joy and song

altering all the seasons so that nature became utterly confused

killing off the flowers and other plants with unexpected frosts

- Two pupils went into role as Titania and Oberon, provided with these statements of grievance.

- Two pupils were given the responsibility of acting as their legal representatives.

- The teacher acted as arbitrator in the debate.

- The rest of the class formed a circle to include Titania and Oberon. The working couple were positioned on opposite sides, each seated with their solicitor.

- The pupils in role as the Fairy King and Queen and their representatives had some time to translate all their grievances into first language.

- The arbitrator established the rules of engagement, which were as follows:

  (a) Oberon would state his grievances, but only in Urdu or Panjabi (the fairies didn't speak English!)

  (b) These grievances would then be translated by his solicitor to the rest of the group, who would be assisting the arbitrator in his final decision.

  (c) The group would have the right to question him through his solicitor, but only on the facts.

  (d) Then the process would be repeated for Titania.

  (e) The whole dispute would then be open to general discussion, regulated by the arbitrator, who would do his best to keep order.

(f) In this general discussion, anyone from the group could ask questions or make comments through the bilingual solicitors.

(g) Oberon and Titania could also make comments and, if they wished, argue with one another across the circle.

(h) When the arbitrator reckoned that the debate had run its course, he would stop proceedings and instruct the complainants to leave the room (with their representatives).

(i) A decision would then be made by the whole group, led by the arbitrator, and the two parties would be asked back to hear the outcome (they would have the right to make a final statement, which again would be issued through their solicitors.)

A typical exchange went like this:

OBERON (in first language):
Look, all I want you to do is to let me have the Changeling Boy.
Then the world can have its seasons back and all the other things.
TITANIA (in first language):
But that's blackmail.
Do you really want the world to carry on suffering like this just because you are jealous of a little boy?
OBERON (in first language):
Look, I'm the Fairy King and I've got the power.
If you want everybody to go on suffering then you keep the boy.
TITANIA (in first language):
So it's now all my fault that there are fogs and floods and famine!
I can't believe you!
ARBITRATOR (in English):
Please can the legal representatives translate what your clients are saying?
(Each solicitor provides a translation).

ARBITRATOR (in English):
Would anyone please like to reply to any of these points or ask Oberon or Titania any questions?
PUPIL A (in English):
Yes. Oberon, why do you want this boy so much?
Can't you see he is making your wife really happy.
Don't you want your wife to be happy?
(This is translated back to Oberon).
OBERON(in first language):
If that boy was my page, she could still see him.
I don't know why she is making all this fuss.
TITANIA (in first language):
If you ever got your hands on that little boy, that would be the last I saw of him.
He only wants him because he makes me happy.
He's jealous of that!
He can't handle it!
(Again this is translated).
PUPIL B (in English):
Has anyone asked what the little boy wants?
Did the Queen take him away against his will?
Is he under her spell?
Perhaps he'd like to go home to his own family and people in India.

This structure extends the idea of hot-seating and applying the idea within a bilingual framework elevates it onto a higher plain, both linguistically and dramatically. It provides all participants with a variety of exciting dramatic options: the exploration of human and environmental issues; the development of the personal conflict between Oberon and Titania; consideration of how disputes between two such uncompromising opponents can be handled and, hopefully, settled.

The bilingual element, as well as making the activity far more interesting and engaging, gives the two solicitors a crucial role. Their ability to translate the feelings of their clients and to act as intermediaries between all the parties is vital to the whole process; it also infuses the improvisation with legal weight.

5
Unravelling Shakespearean sonnets in the multilingual classroom

The Prologue to *Romeo and Juliet*

As part of a more general PHSE topic focusing on relationships and conflicts, a Year 8 class worked with me on some of the themes in *Romeo and Juliet*. The issues of family loyalty and conflict, forced marriages, and the generation conflict within Verona were all wholly relevant.

The starting point was the Prologue, which presents the audience with an overview of the plot. Also, it is written in a sonnet form, providing the opportunity to do some work on the structure and poetic form of a sonnet. To my surprise, I found that asking my pupils to think creatively within such a disciplined literary convention opened unexpected doors.

* In groups of eight, they began with a shared reading of the text:

Two households, both alike in dignity
In fair Verona, where we set our scene,
From ancient grudge break to new mutiny,
Where civil blood makes civil hands unclean.
From the fatal loins of these two foes
A pair of star-crossed lovers take their life,
Whose misadventured piteous overthrows
Doth with their death bury their parents' strife.
The fearful passage of their death-marked love

And the continuance of their parents' rage
Which but their children's end, naught could remove -
Is now the two hours traffic of our stage;
The which if you with patient ears attend,
What here shall miss, our toil shall strive to mend.

- Each group identified the words they found difficult and unfamiliar. For this they were provided with a small glossary.

- Pupils fed back their research and collectively discussed meanings, thus removing any barriers caused by the density of some of Shakespeare's language and syntax.

- With the class divided into three groups, each pupil was given a slip of paper on which was printed a small section of the prologue. These short textual passages were arranged in sequence and adhered to the way Shakespeare had punctuated the opening speech.

- Students took turns reciting their parts. Through this activity they appreciated how Shakespeare's punctuation guided the actor in his interpretation of the speech. Some of the pupils complained that their parts were a bit of a mouthful to read out. They discovered that Shakespearean actors must learn to speak their lines 'on breath', which is not easy. This became a challenge that many of the pupils were eager to take up.

- In their groups, each now arranged in a circle, the pupils recited their lines as they walked across the circle to one another.

- One by one they pronounced the last word in each line – the rhyming words.

- Tableaux were made by each group, representing the rhyming words. After a few rehearsals, the effect of this device became highly dramatic.

- All the groups devised a word in Urdu to resemble the rhyming words in the sonnet. Much stimulating discussion was generated by this activity.

- Having agreed upon their Urdu words, the pupils repeated the previous exercise, but this time echoed the rhyming words in Urdu, immediately followed by the tableaux: the dramatic effect was noticeably improved.

Through these activities, the pupils began to comprehend the significance of the words on which Shakespeare chose to end each line. These words: *dignity, scene, mutiny, unclean, foes, life, overthrows, strife, love, rage, remove, stage, attend, mend* – were charged with special meaning. And the pupils were more easily able to work out the structure of the sonnet from this preparatory work.

- Next they began highlighting all the words that related to conflict.

- Using these words, in twos, they devised a news reading that incorporated the main points and details of the Prologue, in the style of a television news broadcast. This gave them the chance for some code-switching, moving from Shakespearean English into a modern register.

- The best 'broadcasts' were acted out and used as models to help the rest of the group to improve and polish their efforts. This is drama's equivalent of the literary procedure of redrafting. It is essential that in dramatic presentation pupils are given the opportunity to reflect on their work and that of others, as with creative writing; to share and celebrate good practice; and to improve and polish their initial contributions.

- The pupils were informed that this news item was being presented all round the world: 'If this was broadcast in Pakistan, what might it sound like?' They then developed a bilingual version of the news item.

The culmination to all these activities was the creation of an Exhibition of Living Sculptures in the Gallery of Modern Art in Verona: pupils had to imagine that they lived in modern Verona, and that a controversial contemporary artist had decided to depict the main events surrounding the lives of Romeo and Juliet in a series of living statues, using real people rather than clay. These statues would keep changing their shapes during the public presentation.

- Pupils created five tableaux depicting the main phases in the prologue.

- They devised four separate movements for each that would animate their living sculpture.

- Captions in both English and Urdu were agreed upon to represent each phrase, some of them taken directly from the text.

- Each living sculpture rehearsed their presentation. These were then acted out in sequence.

- With the teacher in role as the temperamental artist, alterations and improvements were made to each tableau (which gave me an excuse to make a few changes).

- Group sculptures performed their living tableaux to the accompaniment of Roderigo's Concerto for the Guitar. This injected an emotive strain into their individual pieces and also had the effect of slowing down their movements.

As the icing on the cake, the drama area was later transformed into the exhibition room of the gallery, using the stage blocks, tables, chairs and pieces of material. A class of Year 6 pupils was specially invited for a private showing of this live bilingual art exhibition. Providing an opportunity for older students to perform for a younger audience is a great motivator. It gives the performers a real sense of purpose. There is also far less pressure than when having to perform in front of one's peers. Afterwards, in role as the artist, I asked this specially invited and highly discerning audience for their comments, and made alterations to the tableaux accordingly.

Sonnet 91

Later, the same Year 8 class explored another Shakespearean sonnet. I chose Number 91, because of its simplicity of form and directness of language, which I felt would have a strong impact on the class.

- The class was divided into three groups and all read the poem:

Some glory in their birth, some in their skill,
Some in their wealth, some in their body's force,
Some in their garments (though new-fangled ill)

Some in their hawks and hounds, some in their horse.
And every humour hath his adjunct pleasure
Wherein it finds a joy above the rest.
But these particulars are not my measure;
All these I better in one general best.
Thy love is better than high birth to me,
Richer than wealth, prouder than garment's cost,
Of more delight than hawks or horses be,
And having thee of all men's pride I boast,
Wretched in this alone: that thou may'st take
All this away, and me most wretched make.

- Each group was given copies of the Prologue to *Romeo and Juliet*, as an immediate point of reference, and they compared the rhyming patterns. The similarities were obvious and the understanding of the basic structure of the sonnet was re-inforced. I also pointed out that the majority of sonnets were love poems in which the identity of the subject was protected. This evoked a few questions – having to unravel a possible mystery appealed to everyone.

- In fours, the pupils took turns to read the first four lines of the sonnet according to the way it was punctuated.

- They reflected on Shakespeare's use of repetition in the sonnet and its effect on the reader. Some pupils suggested that it made the start of the poem read rather like a list. The resulting inter-change between teacher and class went something like this:

'So what is the poet listing?'
'What people glory in?'
'According to the first four lines, what kind of things do they glory in?'
'Birth.'
'Why should people glory in that?'
'If they're born into a really rich or famous family... Then they might look down on people.'
'Anything else mentioned that was gloried in?'
'Skill.''Wealth.''Body's force!'

'What does the poet mean by that?'
'Strength. Being hard!'
'Garments.'
'What's another word for that?'
'Clothes.'
'Why should people glory in those?'
'Looking smart. Fashion. Wearing designer labels.'
'What about the fourth line?'
'Hawks, hounds and horses.'
'But people don't boast now about having hawks!'
'But they did in olden times. They'd go hunting with them.'
'You mean everyone owned hawks and did that?'
'No, only very wealthy people. In Saudi, the King owns lots of hawks. When people go riding with a hawk on their arm they look like princes.'
'What about horses and hounds, then?'
'People who have racehorses have to be very rich... Fox hunting is only done by people with lots of money... snobs!'

This process of questioning enabled pupils to grasp Shakespeare's intentions at the opening of the poem.

- In pairs, the pupils traded boasts. They boasted about themselves, speaking in both their first and second languages. Each boast was preceded by the phrase in the sonnet: 'I glory in....' Everyone accompanied their boasts with exaggerated flourishes and much foppish behaviour.

- Boasting bouts were organised. The rest of the pupils were encouraged to cheer and applaud the most exaggerated demonstrations of affectation and exhibitionism. As a way into this activity, the teacher gave a wildly exaggerated demonstration of Elizabethan foppishness and challenged volunteers to outdo him.

- The boasts were written up and used as the basis for an Elizabethan rap, which was later performed in a school assembly.

- In fours, pupils highlighted the phrases they liked best in each of the sonnet's next four lines, notably:

hath his pleasure
joy above the rest
these particulars... not my measure
one general best

- This activity was used to support the next task. The pupils' choices were written up on large sheets of paper. Pupils linked these phrases with their own words so they made sense. One typical amalgam read:

'Everyone hath their own pleasure, but my joy above the rest is none of these particulars because of all the things in the world I love doing most I have one general best which is my feeling for you, which is more important than my finest things'.

- This task connected the pupils' understanding of the opening of the sonnet with its development at the end.

- Half the groups were given lines 1-4 of the sonnet. Then they combined with the other half, who read out lines 8-12.

- The pupils played verbal tennis with these lines and finally a pattern:

Group A: *Some glory in their birth*
Group B: *Thy love is better than high birth to me*

Group A: *Some glory in their wealth*
Group B: *Thy love is richer than wealth*

Group A: *Some glory in their garments*
Group B: *Thy love is prouder than garments cost*

Group A: *Some glory in their hawks and hounds, some in their horse*
Group B: *Thy love has more delight than hawks or horses.*

This fairly simple exercise illustrated to the children how Shakespeare successfully brought together all the strands of the sonnet towards its ending. Consequently, they could see how the last two lines clearly stood on their own:

Wretched in this alone; that thou may'st take
All this away, and me most wretched make.

It was clear to them that the sonnet had a sting in its tail. One pupil aptly compared a sonnet to a joke, observing that they both have a punch-line.

- The pupils dramatised the last couplet. They created a scenario, which involved breaking bad news to a best friend. The bad news was linked directly to the context of the poem.

- In pairs, pupils prepared two improvisations. In the first, the best friend of the poet is approached by the person who is the object of his/her affection in the sonnet. She/he requests the best friend to carry back the message to the poet that 'it's all over'.

- The pupils in role as the go-between do their best to speak up for their friend, using some of the images and statements in the sonnet. For example:

  'Wait a moment. He thinks so much about you. Since seeing you he's given up all his usual pleasures – he doesn't think anymore about his hunting and his fashionable clothes, things he used to enjoy so much. Even money no longer has any value for him. He only thinks of you, night and day!'

- Partners swapped round, the best friend assuming the role of the poet on the receiving end. The person breaking the news did so as sensitively and gently as possible, but this time in first language (if that was not English).

Playing out these scenes revealed the transitory nature of love and relationships, something anticipated at the end of the sonnet. Encouraging pupils to use Panjabi when they were breaking the bad news produced two contrasting reactions in the audience. Some of the improvisations were very comical and gave the encounter an unexpected angle, but others were intimate and personal and produced the opposite effect. When you ask bilingual pupils to move into first language, it isn't simply a matter for them of translating a given text into another language. Also brought to the translation is an immense vocabulary of gesture and intonation that can fundamentally affect the nature of the end product and give it an unexpectedly different shape and form. Language is a powerful vehicle for expressing the whole person.

'Prospero' The Tempest

Many of the pupils participating in this work became so enthusiastic that they wanted to compose their own sonnets, using the internal organisation and structuring of ideas they had identified in the original. Here is one of the best:

People pride themselves in their flash cars,
In their necks and wrists all covered in gold,
In their loud behaviour with their mates in bars,
In the dodgy deals they make with young and old.
In their daily lives, they swagger and strut
Like peacocks squawking with so much noise.
For me the door to that kinda life is now firmly shut
Late nights chatting up girls, chillin out with the boys
Because you, my Angel, are finer than gold,
Sweeter than the sweetest Arabian sherbert
More exciting than risky fortunes won and sold,
The smart style of past friends, of greater worth
And yet, unknown to you, these feelings always rage
Me, far too frightened to tell, again tears up this page.
A.S.

I have also used the *ghazal*, the Urdu counterpart to the Elizabethan sonnet, with my pupils. This poetic form originated in 10th Century Iran and was at its height under the Moghul emperors in India in the 16th Century. I follow the same procedure as I use when working on the sonnets, encouraging the pupils to explore the structure and images of the poem through drama in both in Urdu and English so as to experience the feelings these arouse in the listener and reader.

6

Performing Shakespeare: reaching out to the wider community

There are many ways of developing the experiential drama work the pupils have achieved in the classroom into a theatretical performance.

Drama is an extremely effective vehicle for promoting language and learning, and for enabling pupils to engage intellectually, physically and emotionally with literary texts. Within this active learning framework, there are numerous opportunities for using performance in the intimacy and security of the small working group: it is a useful strategy for gaining feedback, providing encouragement and praise, making constructive evaluations and stimulating reflection.

Transforming drama experience into theatre is a logical progression. Theatre is a unique sphere of creative activity and self-expression, and children take to it with enthusiasm. Building performance employs many of the forms used in experiential drama activities but it is more immediately concerned with having and instilling an awareness of audience. Decisions about dramatic shape, interpretation, delivery of text, movement and gesture, effective use of props, entrances and exits are all important and require young performers to think carefully about what they do. Theatre is a highly disciplined process, requiring its participants to exercise self-control, teamwork and attention to detail.

The performance work I have described was accomplished outside the curriculum; it was the icing on the cake. Performing skills of real quality are best achieved by pupils in schools that integrate drama into the curriculum. Drama work in the classroom acts as scaffolding for promoting theatre. One-off productions after school are less likely to produce quality results or meaningful outcomes – this is dabbling with drama and the performing arts, rather than developing them.

Over a ten year period, our middle school performed versions of a wide range of Shakespeare's plays: *As You Like It, A Midsummer Night's Dream, Twelfth Night, Macbeth, Cymbeline, A Winter's Tale, Romeo and Juliet, Julius Caesar, The Tempest, Antony and Cleopatra* and *Henry IV*. These were successfully staged because of the drama experience the pupils had acquired while working actively with Shakespeare's plays within the curriculum. They had gained the expertise and, more importantly, the confidence to use and communicate Shakespeare's language, and to interpret his plots and characters. Shakespeare – his world and theatre – had become known and familiar territory.

When schools cultivate an interest in Shakespeare (and other great writers) they can carry it to the parents and the wider community. Extending the audience is a primary function of theatre. Making Panjabi and Urdu an integral part of our Shakespearean productions had a powerful impact on our multilingual community and far-reaching effects.

Shakespeare still speaks to a 21st Century audience. In our multilingual society it is valuable to communicate his plays in different voices and languages. In Shakespeare's Globe every section of society, regardless of social background, came to watch his plays. It was part and parcel of popular culture. There were no social or cultural barriers in Elizabethan theatre. The experience was open to all.

Our parents and members of the community knew that when we performed a version of a Shakespeare play, they would be able to access the meaning of the plot even if their English was limited, because significant passages of the play would be performed in Urdu or Panjabi. Our pupils, furthermore, were able to perform Shakespeare in a range of language registers, because they had had regular experience of doing so in their weekly drama work within the curriculum. For monolingual members of the audience, the pupils worked with such expressiveness and animation that the first language passages were effectively conveyed: such was the quality of their non-verbal communication skills.

By staging bilingual Shakespeare productions our school made an important contribution to cultural development in the multicultural community. We introduced Shakespeare to hundreds of people who would never have encountered his plays. We may well have been creating a future audience that would ultimately go to professional productions of his plays.

Here are examples of three of the successful bilingual productions we performed. The way we developed them might offer guidance to teachers hoping to enthuse and educate their pupils about drama and particularly Shakespeare in multi-ethnic and multilingual schools.

Julius Caesar

In 1993, a large group of Year 8 pupils presented *Julius Caesar* in a Schools Shakespeare Drama Festival in West Bradford. The production grew out of the experiential drama work we'd done the previous year as part of the Year 7 curriculum.

We had to limit the performance to 30 minutes, so it had to be very tight. And because there was such a large cast, a performance structure had to be devised that allowed plenty of scope for crowd scenes. *Julius Caesar* is ideal.

We focused on four main scenes:

* Caesar's confrontation with the Soothsayer

* The meeting of Cassius and the other conspirators at Brutus' house

* The murder of Caesar

* Caesar's funeral

The principal challenge of the first scene was to help a large group of pupils organise their movements and order their group reactions so as to create a responsive and volatile atmosphere for Caesar as he left the Forum. One large section of the crowd thought up football-style chants for the conquering hero. These were spoken in Panjabi (Ancient Rome was a very multicultural community!). Others went into role as media people – cameramen, photographers, reporters. The media circus had to decide on tactics for approaching Caesar as he processed through the crowds. Caesar was provided with minders, and they had to formulate an efficient working procedure for getting him safely through the multitudes and identifying likely troublemakers.

Other pupils were in role as Mark Antony (who took charge of the security operation), Cassius and, of course, the Soothsayer.

The pupils acted out Cassius' vivid account to Brutus of what happened when Caesar was offered the kingly crown before the Roman multitude. We followed this sequence:

- Caesar being offered the crown three times by Mark Antony (great scope for bilingual crowd responses and chanting.)

- Caesar being greeted by chanting (in Panjabi) and jostling crowds. Also being approached aggressively by media people on his way (it is the world press, so the media will speak to Caesar in different languages and Caesar will have interpreters).

- Caesar spotting Cassius

- Caesar suddenly being stopped in his tracks by the Soothsayer

- Caesar having an epileptic fit

- Cassius approaching Brutus as the crowds are dispersing

It took much discussion and planning to synchronise and structure all this action. There was a great bustle of activity when Caesar arrived on the scene: people wanting to shake hands, the crowd chanting and making sudden surges, photographers flashing their cameras, reporters trying to do interviews, bodyguards striving to ensure safe passage for Caesar. All this needed careful orchestration. We found that freeze framing and creating tableaux clarified the events; so did having the crowd going into slow motion on given signals.

When the Soothsayer suddenly crossed Caesar's path, all the performers froze. This dramatic pause allowed Caesar and the Soothsayer to act out some of the text in the play. The girl playing the Soothsayer spoke her warnings in Urdu. This heightened the dramatic effect because Caesar had to have her words translated. She created an excellent innovation, throwing a handful of bones (pebbles) on the ground and reading the warning from the pattern formed when they landed. She told me afterwards that the inspiration for this idea had come from an Indian film she'd seen, in which someone conjured up a curse against her rival. Selected extracts from the text of the play were added and acted out at key moments: for example, Caesar observing that Cassius had a lean and hungry look whereas he himself preferred men who are fat.

The pupils used the dialogue they'd previously worked out in improvisation, both in Panjabi and English, for the moment Caesar collapsed with the falling sickness. All this was then structured and polished for actual performance. They acted out Caesar's fit in slow motion, framing at intervals and interjecting it with verbal exclamations and asides.

Juggling all these disparate elements took a great deal of work and rehearsal. There was a good deal of negotiation between me and the cast, and among the members of the cast, before the final scene was resolved. When developing theatrical performance, pupils need to be given as much responsibility as possible for its dialogue and action. The director's role should be to evaluate what the actors created and negotiate over the parts that might need trimming or extending. Ideally, performance should develop naturally out of improvisation. It then becomes the director's task to help the pupils to shape their work with their audience in mind. This method of working gives the pupils a real stake in the development of the production, and makes the whole process more meaningful and relevant.

The meeting of the conspirators
The conspirators' encounter is preceded by a storm, giving scope for a dramatic start to the scene. Some of the cast were equipped with percussion instruments to produce Jove's firework show. The con-

spirators all carried umbrellas as they made their way to Brutus' villa. In the tableaux and framing techniques, these umbrellas were used to great visual effect.

Underpinning the action, each of the conspirators took lines and phrases from Casca's speech describing the extraordinary force and nature of the tempest:

Are you not moved, when all the sway of Earth
shakes like a thing infirm?

I have seen tempests, when the scolding winds
have rived the knotty oaks

And I have seen the ocean swell and rage and foam,
to be exalted with the threatening clouds.

But never till tonight, never till now,
did I go through a tempest dropping fire....
(Act 1 Scene 3 ll 3-10)

The children performed these lines in total darkness; the only light was provided by torches, which they turned up to light up their faces.

So after they knocked on Brutus' door, the conspirators entered his villa with a genuine sense of being windswept, bedraggled and desperate for shelter. The conspirators had improvised their own arguments for persuading Brutus to join their cause in advance, especially over the delicate matter of Caesar's assassination. This kind of role-play helps to bond the group and develop their thinking in the context of the drama. The conspirators had the actual text of this scene, from which they selected lines for themselves that would heighten the effect of the final dialogue.

Next they worked out asides to express what they were thinking to themselves as they tried to entice Brutus to join the conspiracy, for example:

'I don't think he likes that!'

'Supposing he grasses on us all? Will we have to kill him?'

'That seems to have hit the mark! He can't handle the idea that Caesar might destroy the Republic and become a dictator.'

'Maybe Cassius should slow down a bit and give Brutus the chance to get his head round some of these ideas.'

These asides were to be delivered in first language, thereby drawing a bilingual audience into the secret of the conspiracy.

The murder of Caesar

For Caesar's murder, the conspirators were told the sequence of events as presented in the play, commencing with the delegation of senators arriving at Caesar's residence and ending with Mark Antony's dramatic entrance immediately after Caesar's bloody murder.

As a dry run, the group first rehearsed the entire plan. Two pupils went into role as Caesar and Antony, to determine and then practice the kind of movements, gestures and language they would use in the performance. Other members of the cast had roles as hawkers, pick-pockets, street entertainers, beggars and other senators. They created the hurly-burly of inner city Rome as the back-drop for the main action.

The murder itself was stylised and carefully orchestrated, employing techniques of framing and slow motion. As each of the conspirators put in the knife they uttered an exclamation in their first language – again a useful means of connecting the action with a bilingual audience and gaining their attention. The exclamations were along these lines:

'That's for banishing my brother!'

'That's for not giving me my promotion!'

'That's for trying to rob us of our freedom!'

'That's for treating us like slaves!'

'How does it feel to be at our mercy now?'

Using this democratic approach to performance and allowing the pupils themselves to shape the dramatic action through improvisation might be time-consuming, but it is far more rewarding than telling them what to do. It gives pupils ownership of the whole process. It is a dynamic way of working, allowing many opportunities for negotiation and decision-making. It aims at involving every member of the cast and, because each is an integral part of the whole operation, they are all more involved and more skilled when it comes to the final product. It is too easy sometimes for the director to gear everything around the principal characters, who are generally the most talented. This is a soft option and ends with a staging that can be rather wooden and which lacks the energy with which a whole cast can imbue a performance. And the total involvement of the whole class is lost.

Empowering the cast with the right to make its own choices about Shakespearean text is the most exciting and fulfilling aspect of working in this way. When pupils are enabled to decide what they want to do, they tend to select text which is vivid in its imagery and ideally suited to conveying the events and their significance to a younger audience.

Caesar's funeral
For the funeral, the Roman crowd was divided into small groups. Each devised a tableau expressing the mood and feeling of the people. Caesar's body was laid out on a platform and draped with a transparent red cloth. As musical backing for the commencement of the scene, part of the film soundtrack for Francis Ford Coppola's 'Dracula' was used, greatly heightening the tension. Once the tableaux were finalised, the Roman crowd moved mournfully, group by group, into their positions. The soundtrack helped to establish the overall pace of their movements and set the mood for the scene.

The prepared speeches took place on a speaker's platform complete with microphone, so the scene resembled a public meeting as much as a funeral.

The funeral speeches of Brutus and Mark Antony employed a dramatic structure that had proved highly successful in the previous year's classwork. The two pupils in role as the senators delivered their funeral orations, using much of Shakespeare's text, while the Roman crowd either heckled or supported the statements they were making, if possible in their first language – again with the aim of drawing a bilingual audience into the scene. After a few dry runs, decisions were made about what lines to retain. The kind of outcome achieved was as follows (the responses not shown in italics were spoken mostly in Panjabi):

BRUTUS
Romans, countrymen and lovers
We're no lovers of yours! You and your friends killed Caesar!
Hear me for my cause,
Why should we listen, murderer!
And be silent... that you may hear!
Alright, give the man a chance; hear him out!
Believe me for mine honour, and have respect to mine honour,
that you may believe... If there be any in this assembly, any
dear friend of Caesar's, to him I say that Brutus' love to
Caesar was no less than his.
So you killed him! With friends like that, who needs enemies?
If then that friend demand why Brutus rose against Caesar, this
is my answer:
not that I loved Caesar less, but that I loved Rome more...
Nobody could have loved Rome more than Caesar! Look at the battles he fought for us and won! Look at all the treasure he brought into the city!
What are you talking about?
Had you rather Caesar were living and die all slaves, than that
Caesar were dead to live as free men...
We would rather be Caesar's slaves than yours, Brutus! etc.
(Act 3 Scene 2 ll 13 ff)

Manipulating Shakespeare's text like this made the language far more comprehensible to the performers' parents than any conventional staging could have done, and thus the community was drawn into their children's school activity. The interruptions in first language actively engaged their interest and attention and indicated that the school valued and used their language.

The Tempest

Our production of *The Tempest* proved the value of creating a close partnership between different areas in the expressive arts. We wanted to create a dramatic environment that was magical but at times menacing. Under the direction of our music teacher, pupils playing keyboards, xylophones, percussion instruments and sitars conjured up the atmosphere of a becalmed sea, a violent storm and an island which on the one hand:

Is full of noises,
Sounds, and sweet airs, that give delight and hurt not....
(Act 3 Scene 2 ll 138-140)

but which, on the other, can throw up a multitude of sudden and terrifying allusions. The musical effects not only provided the back-drop for the whole production but also enabled the cast to project themselves into the action of the scenes during rehearsals. So much of *The Tempest* is to do with its magical atmosphere, and music and sound proved an effective way of weaving this into the fabric of the performance.

Prospero's long speech to his daughter Miranda at the start of the play, describing his expulsion from Milan by his power-crazed brother Antonio, was made visual. Through a combination of mime and tableaux, a series of flashbacks was produced that mirrored the events set out in Prospero's lengthy account. The dumb show was en-livened by 16th century style harpsichord and organ music on the keyboard, reflecting the changing moods of Prospero's words – moving from his extreme melancholy at the loss of his wife to the more threatening and violent conspiracy being organised against him. The musical accompaniment determined the pace and mood of the mime and the entire sequence visually communicated the mean-ing of a dense Shakespearean text to our bilingual audience.

The role of Caliban was taken by a girl. In the preliminary discus-sions, it was clear that the pupils felt that Caliban was a victim – someone to be pitied rather than scorned. 'What must it be like to have your island home taken away from you and your mother killed?' was a common reaction. Some of the pupils perceptively noted that Caliban had been deprived of his language by his new master, Prospero. This was an issue close to the hearts of our bilingual pupils. Certain of Caliban's lines were particularly poignant:

You taught me language, and my profit on't
Is I know how to curse. The red plague rid you
For learning me your language.
(Act 1 Scene 2 ll 365-367)

These words encapsulate once more how Shakespeare's plays reflect current issues. The girl playing Caliban selected the text she wanted to use and felt she could understand. She combined these gobbits of Shakespearean text with a mixture of 'broken English' and Panjabi, which we decided would be the language of the island. Whenever she used her first language in Prospero's presence, he would punish her, so vividly reflecting the language issue. She also delivered many

'Caliban' The Tempest

of her words in the register of a small child, because, as she observed Caliban 'probably never had the chance of growing up properly.'

In the comic scenes involving Trinculo and Stephano, Caliban's childish innocence was exploited to the full. Caliban used her Panjabi to exaggerate what she thought were the superhuman attributes of these two losers, and this emphasised the comic irony of the situation to a bilingual audience.

Three pupils shared the role of Ariel; she was presented as one figure who had an usual number of heads, arms and legs – achieved by creating the silhouette of the three pupils with an overhead projector behind a white cotton sheet. She looked like the Hindu deity, Durga, which seemed highly appropriate. This device also enabled the character to take a more versatile form. Because all the Ariels wore identical costumes and half masks, they could either appear as a single entity or as separate individuals: the illusion was effectively created of being in more than one place at a time. The three pupils in this role had complimentary talents: one could play the recorder beautifully, another was a talented dancer and the third was very advanced in Urdu. This produced some interesting and diverse effects in performance. For example, when King Alonso of Naples, Antonio and their fellow Milanese castaways found themselves marooned on the island, one of the Ariels lulled them to sleep with the sound of her recorder; another moved expressively (and invisibly) around the group, casting sleeping dust into their eyes; while the third spoke in Urdu some of Ariel's words from the text which she had translated.

Having a collective Ariel created other exciting effects too, especially with the shocking apparition of the Harpy at the magical banquet prepared for Antonio and his fellow Italians. The scene for the meal was presaged by haunting and eerie sounds from the keyboard. The invisible Ariels brought in the plates of food: the castaways conveyed to the audience the idea that in their eyes, the plates were moving by themselves. When the keyboard sounds changed to become high-pitched and exceedingly discordant, the Ariels created their fantastic illusion: one manipulating a large mask on a pole while the other two waved wings, constructed with tissue on light wooden frames. The resultant large puppet-like Harpy was bathed in blood-red light! This proved a spectacular effect and demonstrated the value of occasionally presenting a Shakespearean character by means of more than one actor.

Prospero was depicted as a ruthless and vengeful wielder of power who used his magic to subdue others. Music was the essential manifestation of his sorcery in the production. When Prospero broke his staff at the conclusion of the play, it was as if a conductor had snapped his baton.

With this gesture, a sudden silence descended upon the island – whether peaceful or disconcerting was left to the imagination of the audience.

As You Like It

In summer 1992, our school, three other middle schools and four upper schools participated in a memorable Shakespeare project organised by the Royal Shakespeare Company's Education Programme. This gave us a unique opportunity for exploring *As You Like It* with a group of thirty Year 8 pupils. I've always found the plot of this play rather unwieldy and initially I feared that the meanderings of its storyline might not appeal to thirteen year olds. I was proved wrong; and as the project progressed, I came to love the play more myself.

Far from being put off by all the comings and goings of the play, the pupils were intrigued by them and enjoyed its complexities. We also had the benefit of an initial stimulus provided by Fiona Lindsay, RSC Education Officer, and Lesley Hutchinson, choreographer for David Thacker's production of *As You Like It* that year, who each led a workshop at our school. Through their direction, the essential elements in the story of danger and treachery at court, loyalty and friendship, escape and refuge came across well. Using movement and sound work, tableaux and small group improvisation, all the pupils lived through these experiences. The intensely active and physical approach to the text aroused their interest in the language of the play. The method of pinpointing particular words that conveyed strong images, and, through movement and sound, projecting these in short but vivid improvisations was tremendously effective.

The climax to the project was the trip to Stratford to see the Royal Shakespeare Company's production. This experience of live theatre in such a setting had an impact upon our students in terms of their understanding of the play and its application. It fired their imaginations, as their later comments at school revealed:

'It was a play of darkness and light.'

'In the court, the people moved about like aliens – it was a bit like Star Trek.'

'If I'd been Rosalind, I don't think I could have remained friends with Celia after what her father had done to my dad.'

'What the hell was Oliver's problem – that was his own brother he wanted to kill.'

'I couldn't really understand any of Touchstone's jokes, but I still laughed – I don't know why!'

'I just can't believe how dumb Orlando was that he couldn't recognise Rosalind in the forest. Anybody could see she was a girl.'

'Didn't that Jacques carry on! He was such a sad moaner.'

'Phoebe was a total pain. How could Silvius fancy her? He must have been really stupid!'

One of the big issues arising from this discussion was an environmental one: the need to protect and preserve natural resources like rain forests. Somebody in the group posed the question:

Do people behave better in natural places like forests than they do in towns and cities which have been man-made? ... There's more murder and violence in a city than there is in a rainforest.

I found myself under growing pressure from Year 8 to work towards an end of term production. During our preliminary improvisation work, we decided to make a few changes to clarify the story for a younger audience. We added some scenes of our own and cut out others which we felt could be confusing. For example, at the beginning of the play, the pupils improvised Duke Senior's return to the palace, where he discovered his brother's heavies waiting for him with orders for his immediate expulsion. They portrayed the courtier Le Beau as a man caught between the loyalty of two masters. They also had Frederick's henchmen denying the Duke access to his own daughter, Rosalind – even preventing his saying his last goodbyes to her. A powerful confrontation between Rosalind and her treacherous uncle ensued, in which she demanded an explanation of her father's whereabouts, with her cousin Celia daring to take Rosalind's side against her own father.

Exploring a Shakespearean play with pupils in this open-ended way allows everyone to enter the world he created with his characters and settings; one is given the liberty to live out the story in one's own way. This is the value of adopting a storymaking approach to Shakespeare's plays. It allows many opportunities for pupils to re-invent them in ways that carry special meanings for them.

Inspired by David Thacker's production at Stratford, Duke Frederick's court was enveloped in a moody and menacing atmos-phere (using keyboards and percussion), the courtiers moving in and out of dark corners rather like robotic beings in a sci-fi film. The pupils formed menacing tableaux around Rosalind and Celia, em-phasising their vulnerability.

In the wrestling scene, the cast wanted an extra fight on stage to show the invincibility of the Duke's champion, Charles. In the actual performance, the sight of Charles overwhelming his first opponent heightened the dramatic tension in preparation for the moment when Orlando presented himself from the back of the audience, to respond to what seemed an impossible challenge. The interrogation of Oliver, Orlando's two-faced brother, by Duke Frederick, was portrayed as a scene of Tudor torture. All this engendered an atmosphere of panic and physical menace in the first half of the play. It made Rosalind's and Celia's flight appear more desperate and imperative.

The second half of the play was played bilingually. The inhabitants of the Forest of Arden, such as Corin, Phoebe and Silvius, spoke in Panjabi. The romantic misunderstandings between Rosalind, mas-querading as the boy Ganymede, took on new angle with the lan-guage difference. For this passage of the story, the language mismatch highlighted the cultural divisions between court and country, as well as exacerbating all the comical misunderstandings being acted out in the forest.

Two characters in the play proved a real challenge: Touchstone and Jacques. The girl playing the jester Touchstone was given licence to use her own stock of jokes throughout the performance. The language difference in the Forest of Arden added to the comedy. In the scene where Touchstone and the shepherd Corin are discussing the contrasting merits of life in court and the country, a heated debate was introduced, with much banter and backchat. One of Duke Senior's outlaws became the interpreter in this good-natured dispute, as someone who had lived in the forest long enough to pick up the language of its inhabitants. The odds were stacked against Touchstone because Corin was backed up by a gang of fellow shepherds. The text from the play, spoken by Touchstone, was used as the stimulus to trigger the shepherds' retorts in Panjabi:

CORIN (speaking in Panjabi)
And how like you this shepherd's life, Master Touchstone?
(translated by the interpreter into English)

TOUCHSTONE
Truly, Shepherd, in respect of itself, it is a good life; but in respect that it is a shepherd's life, it is naught. (translated by the interpreter into Panjabi)

THE SHEPHERDS (speaking in their Panjabi version)
'Nothing!' What does he mean by that?
And what does he do all day, tell stupid jokes that no one can understand!
Is that all he learnt in his precious court? (translated by the interpreter to Touchstone in English)

TOUCHSTONE
No. Let me continue!
In respect that a shepherd's life is solitary, I like it very well.
(translated)

THE SHEPHERDS (speaking in their Panjabi)
Oh, so our life is not so bad after all!

Wait a moment, he only likes it when he's on his own!
Is he saying that he doesn't like our company?
Coming from court he thinks he's too good for us. (again
translated)

TOUCHSTONE
In respect that your life is private, it is very vile. (translated)

SHEPHERDS (in their Panjabi)
Vile! That means something really nasty.
Our lives can't be as bad as what goes on in court.
Anyway if court is such a fine place, why are most of the
people who once lived there coming here to Arden instead?
(translated)

TOUCHSTONE
Now in respect it is in the fields, it pleaseth me well!
(translated)

SHEPHERDS (in their own Panjabi)
Oh please, make up your mind!
Do you like it here or not?
I think you are just trying to wind us all up! (translated)

TOUCHSTONE
But (a lot of heckling from the shepherds!)............
In respect it is not in court, it is tedious! (translated)

SHEPHERDS (in their Panjabi)
Tedious! That means boring!
So you think our beautiful forest is boring!
We suppose you think that we are all boring as well!
Thank you! (translated)

TOUCHSTONE
As it is a spare life, look you, it fits my humour well (again
much heckling)
*But as there is no more plenty in it, it goes much against my
stomach.* (translated)

SHEPHERDS (in their Panjabi)
'Spare life' – so you don't think any of the time you are

spending in our forest is important?
As for humour, we've had enough of all your so-called jokes!
'Plenty'? Plenty of what? If you mean money, we don't need it here.
We have everything that god gives us.
As for stomach – we've noticed that a lot of the people in court have large ones! Not enough exercise, eh! (translated)

TOUCHSTONE
Hast any philosophy in thee, shepherds? (translated)

The same framework was adopted for Corin's reply:

CORIN
No more but that I know the more he sickens, the worse at ease he is, and that he that wants money, means, and content is without three good friends; that the property of rain is wet, and fire to burn; that good pasture makes fat sheep; and that a great cause of the night is lack of sun.
(Shakespeare text taken from Act 3 Scene 2 ll 11 ff)

This passage was not too difficult to translate into first language. Like Touchstone's speech, it was broken down into one-liners, with the shepherds speaking them in turn. The interpreter again acted as go-between. There was enough scope for the sharp Touchstone to make fun of these comments and extend the good-humoured banter. In this way, Shakespeare's dialogue was accessed much more readily by a bilingual audience.

As for Jacques, the young man who took the part had a dry, off-beat sense of humour that was tailor-made for the role. The seven ages of man speech starting with the famous lines:

All the world's a stage...

he insisted on doing in its entirety. In rehearsals he made such a song and dance about his performance that Duke Senior's band of outlaws spontaneously started heckling him. This proved lively a piece of theatre that was included in the eventual performance. The production also made much of the scene in which the deer was killed and – following the interpretation in the Stratford production – Jacques reacted with distress to the brutality of the hunt, so revealing a sensitive side to his character. A large sack was filled and splashed with red paint to represent the carcass of the dead deer. Two pupils in the cast were vegetarians, so this scene prompted heated discussion.

Music became an important element in the second half of the play. The music teacher rewrote the music of Blow, Blow thou Winter Wind, to produce a more contemporary sound. The girl playing Amiens, Duke Senior's minstrel, had a glorious voice. She was accompanied by three backing vocalists (all of whom were fellow outlaws). The effect of her song and its beautiful lyrics was striking:

Blow, blow, thou winter wind,
Thou art not so unkind
As man's ingratitude.
Thy tooth is not so keen,
Because thou art not seen,
Although thou breath be rude.
Hey-ho, sing hey-ho unto the green holly,
Most friendship is feigning, most loving, mere folly.
Then hey-ho the holly;
Life is most jolly.
Freeze, freeze, thou bitter sky,
That dost not bite so nigh
As benefits forgot.
Though thou the waters warp,
Thy sting is not so sharp
As friend remembered not.
Hey-ho, sing hey-ho unto the green holly.
Most friendship is feigning, most loving, mere folly.
Then hey-ho the holly;
Life is most jolly.
(Act 2 Scene 7 ll 174-194)

The song was sung while the rest of the outlaws huddled together around the remnants of a camp-fire, covered in blankets. Duke Senior's band of loyal friends assumed the character of refugees – and the lyrics of the song highlighted everyone's personal sense of hurt and loss, caused by the treachery and betrayal of others; some-thing much sharper and more painful than the deprivations of their new, harsher forest environment.

The cross-dressing element in the play also worked to our advantage. Whereas Shakespeare had boys playing female roles, some of the main male characters in our production were played by girls – an interesting reversal. This greatly assisted the subtle exchanges bet-ween Rosalind (disguised as Ganymede) and Orlando, her love-struck suitor; it also helped Celia and Oliver's bonding near the end of the play, removing any potential embarrassment which might have been caused if boys had been playing the roles of the two young men. The casting liberated the girls, enabling them to work in a more focused and uninhibited way on Shakespeare's language and the intricacies of his dramatic situations.

The most memorable aspect of this particular production was the ability of our students to code-switch. Their capacity to move from their spoken English into Shakespeare's language, then into either Panjabi or Urdu, and then yet again into everyday English, was quite extraordinary. As a result, a most difficult Shakespearean play – one that normally would not be attempted by a group of 13 year olds – was successfully presented to a multilingual audience. It gave them an entreé to a play that they might never normally have had the chance to experience.

'Tom foolery' downstairs! Twelfth Night

7

Leading bilingual pupils into Shakespeare's world

In his monumental book *Shakespeare: the invention of the human,* Harold Bloom wrote:

> We keep returning to Shakespeare because we need him; no one gives us so much of the world most of us take to be fact.

and:

> You can bring absolutely anything to Shakespeare and the plays will light it up.

Bloom thus emphasises the value and importance of introducing pupils to Shakespeare's plays from an early age. The plays continue to inform our times about the great universal issues. They touch upon what is essentially human in all of us; no other writer has better reproduced the human spirit in all its multiplicity of forms, both noble and ignoble, and with such originality and power. In terms of my personal teaching, working on Shakespeare's plays and stories has always enhanced the quality of the learning experience of children and intensified the level of pupil response. This has much to do with the uniqueness of Shakespeare's characters and the abiding appeal and universality of his stories. It is due also to his rich, sensuous, colourful and memorable language.

It was once suggested to me that my work on Shakespeare was a waste of time. 'What's the point doing Shakespeare with these children? How can his plays be relevant to any children living in the

1990s, let alone those coming from a completely different culture?'
The assertion was that Shakespeare's plays described a totally different world and had nothing to do with the 20th century: 'They'll
only confuse our kids!' This view was dismally patronising and revealed low expectations of bilingual pupils. The main grounds on
which such criticism of studying Shakespeare in school was based –
its 'otherness' and seeming 'irrelevance' – are precisely the reasons
for studying Shakespeare, particularly with bilingual pupils from
diverse cultural backgrounds.

Rex Gibson, Editor of the Cambridge School Shakespeare and a
pioneer in the field of Shakespeare in school, wrote in 1998 that:

> A powerful argument for studying Shakespeare exists in his
> extraordinariness, his strangeness, his unfamiliarity. His appeal
> lies in a unique blend of the familiar and the strange, his rele-
> vance and his remoteness. All education is about opening doors,
> extending opportunities and experience. It is concerned that
> individuals should not be imprisoned in a single point of view,
> confined solely to local knowledge and beliefs. Education
> shows that there is a world elsewhere beyond the familiar and
> everyday... Shakespeare's characters express themselves in
> heightened language, and live in worlds that are clearly not those
> of today.

My bilingual pupils have been intrigued by the new worlds presented
in Shakespeare's stories. Because they have explored them through
active drama experience, they have been able to act out the anxieties,
dilemmas, joys and miseries of a whole range of Shakespearean
characters. Prospero's island, King Lear's Albion, Romeo and Juliet's
Verona, *Twelfth Night's* Illyria, the Forest of Arden in *As You Like It*,
Hamlet's Elsinore have all captured their imaginations and opened
new worlds to them. Studying Shakespeare has created endless
opportunities for acquiring fresh insights into life and the human
condition. Pupil learning should not be limited to the humdrum and
everyday; children need, and deserve, wider experience. The huge
popularity of Tolkein's *The Hobbit* and *Lord of the Rings* cycle, as
well as the recent Harry Potter books, demonstrates the need children have to escape from their everyday lives and experience the un-

chartered realms of the imagination, where there are few constraints and anything is possible. As Robert Witkin (1974) puts it:

> There is a world that exists beyond the individual, a world that exists whether or not he (sic) exists... The child needs to know about this world and manage himself in it... It is a world of facts, of public space and objects... But there is another world, however, a world that exists only because the individual exists. It is the world of his own sensations and feelings... the world of private space and the solitary subject.

Shakespeare offers that other world to the pupil in a unique way. The world in which Hamlet resides is a world of a solitary subject occupying that private space, struggling to come to terms with a troubled and troubling human situation. It is not surprising that critics such as Harold Bloom regard Shakespeare as peerless among writers in his ability to express the humanity that lies within us all. Exposing pupils to Shakespeare's stories raises them to new levels of awareness and consciousness. Peter Brook, in his lecture on Prospero asks:

> ... Does Shakespeare indicate to us... a way to follow, in the same way that *The Mahabharata* maps out a journey for an individual to see the truth? Do Shakespeare's plays... show us the way in which we should be going, the direction we should be facing?

Shakespeare's plays are imbued with the sense that there is something more, some indefinable truth, that lies beyond them. This is especially true of the tragedies like *Hamlet* and *Lear*. I've always felt that this is a journey I want my pupils to take. Through drama experience, Shakespeare's plays can stimulate pupils' philosophical thinking and reflection. Significantly, Brook refers to the great Hindu epic, *The Mahabharata*, which takes a young man training to be a king on a journey of enlightenment which eventually leads him to an understanding of the nature of the living process itself. As Brook points out, there are echoes of this in *The Tempest,* where Prospero was once a young Duke sitting in libraries reading about philosophy, astrology and other mystical issues, but with little idea of what it means to be a ruler. He has to acquire that understanding later from years of exile on his island. Brook makes a fascinating cross-cultural link between a great work of eastern literature and a Shakespearean play, and we can learn much from such connections and comparisons.

The key that can unlock the door to Shakespeare's extraordinary, exciting and thought-provoking world is active drama experience. The language skills of pupils who are bilingual enhance this experience even more.

Drama experience and code-switching
Bilingual pupils are consummate code-switchers. For children who regularly switch from everyday English into Panjabi, back into English and then possibly into Urdu, Elizabethan English becomes another language to move to and from.

The work of educational thinkers such as Cummins and Swaine (1986) and Collier (1989) demonstrates that bilingual learners who have a good level of fluency and conceptual development in their first language can transfer effectively and smoothly to their second and third languages. Evidence shows that when bilingual pupils code-switch, they are using each language independently; the languages do not interfere with one another. Bilingual pupils do not make a conscious translation from one language to another; they move naturally and almost unconsciously between them.

The capacity to code-switch in this fashion is a gift children who can acquire more than one language have early in their language development; having to learn another language after this formative period of language acquisition becomes more difficult.

As I suggested at the start of this book, it may be that bilingual pupils, as skilled code-switchers, rise to the challenge of Shakespeare's dense and complex language better than most monolingual pupils. But this can only happen if the teacher creates a learning environment in which their first language is actively valued and, most importantly, used. Drama is the ideal learning vehicle for making this possible.

Drama, in all its different forms (role-play, mime, forum theatre, tableau, hot-seating etc.), has an infinite capacity for stimulating creative thought and action. Pupils are constantly placed in situations in which they need to solve problems, resolve dilemmas, predict what might happen next through their actions, and project themselves into the minds of the protagonists they are trying to be. Being asked to respond in such a way to Shakespeare – his characters, situations and imagery – can project them in to an exhilarating and dynamic experience. Being encouraged to respond in one's first language can open new doors of experience, perception and understanding.

No learning medium surpasses drama in providing bilingual pupils with opportunities to use code-switching abilities. The fact that they are involved in setting up real language situations means that bilingual students find themselves using their first and second languages to real purpose; and Shakespeare's plots produce many scenarios in which this can happen. Forming relationships, conveying feelings, persuading someone to do something, informing an individual or group, expressing disapproval, encouraging or sympathising, admonishing, deceiving, confusing, expressing humour – all are prime purposes for using language: a character like Iago employs every one of these language devices in the course of his villainy! Shakespeare offers great scope for personal language development through drama, particularly if pupils can use more than one language. Drama also provides an effective medium for pupils to move between different language registers: to experiment with accent, tone, pitch, pace and appropriate vocabulary. Characters like Autolycus, Iago or Falstaff do this many times during the course of a play, responding to the different demands and needs of their various audiences.

When I've observed bilingual pupils developing a Shakespearean situation in their first language, I have always been struck by the expressiveness of their role-play. Seeing the same scene acted out in their everyday English does not have quite the same effect: it is not as animated or natural. In the first language, the use of body language becomes more uninhibited; facial expressions come alive;

intonation and gesture are used less self-consciously and to much greater effect and comic timing is often superb. It's as if all the chains have suddenly been removed, enabling bilingual pupils to be themselves. Experiencing Shakespeare on their own terms through a language in which they can feel themselves appears to be remarkably empowering.

The other hugely liberating aspect of this way of working is the manner in which bilingual pupils use phrases of Shakespeare and everyday English in their first language improvisations. Panjabi is one language that is ideal for code-switching. It often borrows English words, expressions and idioms. Bilingual pupils can use these code-switching opportunities as comic or dramatic devices to achieve greater impact and elicit greater response from an audience.

Experiential drama provides pupils with an audience for their creativity. This audience informs their thinking and allows positive feedback and constructive evaluation: it is essential to the whole dramatic process. Enabling bilingual pupils to communicate in a language they can use skilfully and expressively gives their first language a high profile in the classroom and builds their self-esteem. The most effective learning takes place in pupils who have a sense of self-worth: valuing the language is also valuing the child.

Lastly, there is the power of Shakespeare's language. As Rex Gibson (1998) says:

> Shakespeare's language is both a model and a resource for students. In its blend of formality and flexibility it offers unlimited opportunities for students' own linguistic growth.

This is true for all pupils, bilingual or not. A girl who played Mark Antony in our version of *Julius Caesar* said, after she had performed the beginning of his funeral oration: 'The words were so strong that they made me feel really important up there on stage'. Shakespeare's language has that effect for the actor – that's why actors continue to want to perform his plays. Shakespeare's language empowers the speaker. Enabling bilingual pupils to use their first language alongside Shakespeare's is also very affirming

In the words of Adrian Blackledge (1994): 'To deny (bilingual) children their language is to deny them their story'.

It is of fundamental importance that when bilingual pupils enter the world of Shakespeare's stories, they do so as part of their own story. How else could they make sense of Shakespeare or develop their personal meanings? Jerome Bruner (1987) reports on a similar linguistic enrichment:

> Working in Senegal a few years ago, Dr Greenfield of our laboratory tried an informal little experiment in which she got the children to play guessing games in French and Wolof, and noticed... the richness of the guesses in Wolof and their poverty in French. Not that the French language isn't rich in its capacity, but for the Wolof child it was lacking in its web of associations and fantasies.

> A language that you have never been happy in, never been angry in... a language that is only for school, is no language in which to develop the enterprises of the mind.

This book has tried to describe the remarkable facility that bilingual pupils have to recreate Shakespearean situations in their first language, and the expressiveness and energy they bring to these improvisations. Perhaps it is their first language that enabled them to use that extensive web of personal associations and fantasies. Language is more than just a means of communicating ideas and purposes; it is an integral part of our very being and individuality. Shakespeare's language embodies this reality. This is why, as Bloom (1999) asserts, every succeeding generation needs him and he continues to light up their experience of the world.

For this to happen for bilingual pupils, their first languages have to be brought into the classroom and onto the stage. If teachers make this happen, the whole learning environment is enhanced and transformed for bilingual and monolingual children alike.

Bibliography

Blackledge, Adrian (1994) *Teaching Bilingual Children*, Stoke on Trent, Trentham Books

Bloom, Harold (1999) *Shakespeare: The Invention of the Human*, New York, Riverhead Books

Boal, Augusto (1979) *Theatre of the Oppressed* trans. by Charles A. and Maria-Odilia Leal McBride, Pluto, London

Bolton, Gavin (1995) (with Dorothy Heathcote) *Drama for Learning; Dorothy Heathcote's Mantle of the Expert Approach to Education*, New Jersey, Heinemann

Brook, Peter (1995) *The Quality of Mercy,* London, Temenos Academy

Bruner, Jerome (1986) *Actual Minds, Possible Worlds*, London, Harvard University Press

Bruner, Jerome (1987) quoted in *West Africa Magazine* 9th March 1987

Clark, Jim, Dobson, Warwick, Goode, Tony and Neelands, Jonathon (1997) *Lessons for the Living: Drama and the Integrated Curriculum,* Ontario, Mayfair Cornerstone

Collier, Virginia (1989) How Long? A synthesis of Research on Academic Achievement in a Second language (*TESOL Quarterley* Vol. 23 No. 23 1989)

Cummins, Jim (1994) Knowledge, Power and Identity in Teaching English as a Second Language, in Genesee, F (ed) Educating Second Language Children, Cambridge, Cambridge University Press

Cummins, Jim and Swain, M (1986) *Bilingualism in Education*, Harlow, Longman

Gibson, Rex (1998) *Teaching Shakespeare,* Cambridge, Cambridge University Press

Neelands, Jonathon (1984) *Making Sense of Drama: A Guide to Classroom Practice,* Oxford, Heinemann Educational Books

O'Neill, Cecily C. and Lambert, Alan (1982) *Drama Structures: A Practical handbook for Teachers*, London, Stanley Thornes.

Vygotski, Lev (1938 orig; trans by Michael Cole *et al* 1978) *Mind in Society: the development of the higher psychological processes*, Cambridge, Massachussetts University Press

Witkin, Robert (1974) *The Intelligence of Feeling*, London, Heinemann